PROPHETS OF THE Old Testament

E. Keith Howick

Books by E. Keith Howick

Prophets of the Old Testament

The *Challenged by the Restoration* Series

Challenged by the Old Testament
Challenged by the New Testament
Challenged by the Book of Mormon
Challenged by the Doctrine and Covenants
Challenged by Church History

The *Life of Jesus the Messiah* Series

The Miracles of Jesus the Messiah
The Parables of Jesus the Messiah
The Sermons of Jesus the Messiah
The Mission of Jesus the Messiah
*The Second Coming of Jesus the Messiah**
(*Notable Book Award, 2004 Writers Notes Book Awards)

The *Index* to the *History of the Church of Jesus Christ of Latter-day Saints*

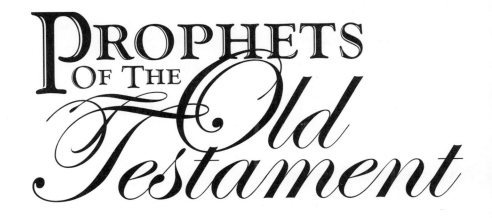

PROPHETS OF THE Old Testament

E. Keith Howick

WindRiver Publishing, Inc.
Silverton, Idaho

Queries, comments or correspondence concerning this work should be directed to the author and submitted to WindRiver Publishing at:

Authors@WindRiverPublishing.com

Information regarding this work or other works published by WindRiver Publishing, Inc., and instructions for submitting manuscripts for review for publication, can be found at:

www.WindRiverPublishing.com

Prophets of the Old Testament

Copyright ©2005 by E. Keith Howick
Cover Design by David Van Etten
"Elijah and the Shunamite Woman" ©2005 by David Van Etten

WindRiver Publishing, the WindRiver Brand Logo, and the WindRiver Windmill Logo are trademarks of WindRiver Publishing, Inc.

Library of Congress Control Number: 2005906012
ISBN-13 978-1-886249-32-5
ISBN-10 1-886249-32-6

First Printing 2005

Printed in the U.S.A. by Malloy, Inc., on acid-free paper

*To my wife, Gail — for her pa-
tience, her support, her inspiration,
her courage, and her perserverance.*

Table of Contents

Prophets of the Old Testament

Prophets of the Old Testament

Alphabetical List of Prophets

Introduction

W hen we hear the word "prophet," we usually think of some one who foretells the future or prophesies about it. Although that is one of the things a prophet may do, it is not the only thing he (and occasionally she) does. A prophet teaches, preaches, calls to repentance, corrects moral wrongs, elucidates religious truths, and from time to time, prophesies. He denounces sin and announces the punishment attributable to it. He is a spokesperson for God, authorized to speak in His name and make His will known to humankind.

The prophets of the Old Testament taught both by word and deed; their actions at times a spiritual "show and tell" of what God had in mind. "The ordinary Hebrew word for prophet is *nabi*, derived from a verb signifying 'to bubble forth' like a fountain; hence the word means one *who announces* or *pours forth* the declarations of God."[1]

Generally speaking, almost everyone classifies the prophets of the Old Testament into major and minor prophets. The four major prophets are Isaiah, Jeremiah, Ezekiel, and Daniel; the minor prophets comprise Hosea, Joel, Amos, Obadiah, Jonah, Micah, Nahum, Habakkuk, Zephaniah, Haggai, Zechariah, and

---

[1] Smith's Bible Dictionary: Prophet.

Malachi— sixteen in all, whose names grace a like number of Old Testament books. The division is not founded on whether any one of the sixteen prophets named is greater or more important than another, but rather on the length of their books. However, this is an artificial classification which may limit the number of prophets to those who wrote books, thereby omitting many others.

There are many prophets identified in the Old Testament. In addition, there are multiple false prophets either referred to generally or identified by name. Even King Saul was once spoken of as a prophet which created the proverb, "Is Saul also among the prophets?"[2] In fact, all men and women in the Old Testament who spoke for and in behalf of the Lord while under the influence of the Spirit can and should be referred to as a prophet or a prophetess, whether they are prophesying, teaching, reproving, or merely delivering a message.

This book is divided into an Introduction, seven Sections, and forty-one Chapters. Once Israel is divided into two kingdoms, some of the prophets minister to both the Northern and Southern Kingdoms. Those prophets are treated in the section where most of their ministries were served. Generally speaking, the scriptural quotes used in the chapters come from the references cited at the beginning of each chapter. Other scriptural and bibliographical references are cited only in footnotes.

There are four charts containing factual information about the prophets and one that identifies the lost books of the Old Testament. There is also one map that shows the various routes (thought to be potential alternate routes) used by the children of Israel as they traveled in the wilderness after the Exodus. Following the name of each prophet is the approximate date that he or she lived or served.

---

[2] 1 Samuel 10:12.

✦ ✦ ✦

This book is *about* the prophets: who they were, what they did, when they lived (as accurately as those dates can be determined),[3] where they came from, where they went, their personalities, their ministries, and what their mission's were—in other words, their *stories*.

God speaks through prophets. Amos states definitively that, "Surely the Lord God will do nothing, but he revealeth his secret unto his servants the prophets."[4] Some Old Testament prophets were accepted, some counseled with, some feared, some rejected, some arrested, some imprisoned, some tortured, some killed, and some enslaved. Because God has given us free agency, we have a choice—to believe and follow the prophets, to disbelieve and reject them, or to ignore them. But what *we* do, has nothing to do with whether God has empowered His prophets. Prophets affect everything and everyone. To say that they are important is an understatement; to say that they are always believed is an overstatement. But to say that they *are,* is an absolute. Read and enjoy *Prophets of the Old Testament.*

Prophets of the Old Testament

---

[3] Dates are either taken from Smith's Bible Dictionary or determined as best as possible from the kings surrounding the time of their ministry. [4] Amos 3:7.

A Man of God out of Judah & The Old Prophet from Bethel

circa 975–954 B.C.
1 Kings 12:25–33; 13:1–32; 2 Kings 23:15–18

There are fifty-seven prophets or groups of prophets in the Old Testament who are identified in one way or another.[5] Let me introduce two of them whose stories are rather bizarre. They appear when Jeroboam was made king of the Northern Kingdom (or Kingdom of Israel), about 975 B.C. Soon thereafter, he became concerned that his people would go up to worship at the temple in Jerusalem and decide to become subjects of Rehoboam, who ruled the Kingdom of Judah. To keep this from happening, Jeroboam made two golden calves and built altars before them so that his priests could burn incense and offer sacrifices in his domain. He placed these golden calves in the geographical extremes of his kingdom—one in Dan and the other in Bethel—and designated them as gods. He appointed his own priests and excluded those from the tribe of Levi. The people were commanded to pay homage to these calf-like gods, to accept Jeroboam's priests, and to recognize Dan and Bethel as their official places of worship and sacrifice. Once the golden calves and altars were installed, the king "ordained" a feast for the people. Upon the

---

[5] There are several prophets mentioned in the Book of Mormon who lived during Old Testament times. Although some of those records were available to the Book of Mormon people, they are not dealt with here because they are not mentioned in the Old Testament itself.

day of the feast, he burned incense and offered sacrifice on the altar at Bethel. In doing these things, Jeroboam committed a great sin.

While Jeroboam was worshiping at the altar in Bethel, the Lord sent an unnamed prophet the scriptures refer to as the *man of God out of Judah* to him to censure him for his idolatrous practices. This unnamed prophet condemned the golden altars and prophesied that a child named Josiah would arise out of the house of David, destroy the wicked priests, and desecrate the altar of Jeroboam by burning dead men's bones upon it. As a sign that his prophecies would come to pass, he said the altar would immediately be broken open and the ashes of past offerings "poured out" or scattered upon the ground.

The *man of God out of Judah* made these prophecies just as Jeroboam placed his hands upon the altar. Jeroboam listened to the prophecies, took one hand from the altar, and pointed his finger toward the man of God, bellowing, "Lay hold on him." But instead of the prophet being detained, three successive miracles occurred. First, the hand Jeroboam used to point to the man of God "dried up," and he could not return it to his side. Second, the altar was rent apart and the ashes it contained were poured out upon the ground. Jeroboam was astonished and must have been contrite, because he begged the man of God to pray for him and restore his hand to normal. The man of God offered a prayer and the third miracle occurred when Jeroboam's hand was restored.

In gratitude, King Jeroboam asked the man of God to dine with him and receive a reward for his services. But the man of God refused, declaring that he had been told by the Lord that he could neither eat nor drink in that "place" (Bethel), and must depart, which he immediately did. Having learned little or nothing from these miraculous experiences, Jeroboam was soon back to his idolatrous ways.

The story now introduces the unnamed *old prophet from Bethel.* This prophet's sons tell him about the strange happenings in Bethel and the prophecies of the *man of God out of Judah.* The old prophet pursues the man of God and finds him resting in the shade of an oak tree. The *old prophet from Bethel* invites the man of God to come with him and eat, to which the *man of God out of Judah* repeats that he must not eat nor drink in this "place." But lying to the man of God, the prophet from Bethel tells him that an angel has sent him to bring the man of God back so that he can be refreshed by food and drink. The *man of God out of Judah* believes the lie of the prophet from Bethel and accompanies him to his lodgings. After the meal, the *old prophet from Bethel* turns around and condemns the *man of God out of Judah* for disobeying the commandment not to eat or drink in Bethel and states that as a result, the man of God's remains would not rest in the sepulcher of his fathers. This prophecy was promptly fulfilled, for as the *man of God out of Judah* left Bethel, he was attacked by a lion and killed. Strangely, the donkey the man of God was riding—along with the killer lion—were found stoically standing guard over the body.

When the *old prophet from Bethel* heard of the man of God's death, he retrieved the body and buried it in his own sepulcher. He even requested that when he died, his body be laid to rest next to the dead man of God—concluding that all that the *man of God out of Judah* had prophesied would surely come to pass

But that's not the end of the story . . . .

Many years later, just as foreseen by the *man of God out of Judah,* the child Josiah is born into the house of David and eventually becomes the king in Judah. In his attempt to restore true worship to all Israel, he destroys the altar at Bethel, takes bones from the sepulchers there, and burns them upon the altar—thus polluting it and fulfilling the prophecies of the *man of God out of Judah.* Josiah sees a title over another sepulcher and asks whose sepulcher it is. He is told that it is the sepulcher of the man of God who had prophesied all that had taken place. Josiah orders that the sepulcher not be disturbed. Thus, the bones of the *man of God out of Judah* and the bones of the *old prophet from Bethel* remained undisturbed . . . perhaps even to this day.

Section I
The Prophet-Patriarchs

The stories of the Patriarchs are contained in the book of Genesis. The complete title of Genesis is: *THE FIRST BOOK OF MOSES, CALLED GENESIS.* It begins with the creation of the earth and ends with the death of Joseph, who was the son of Jacob (or Israel) that was sold into Egypt by his brothers.

Patriarch means "father of a tribe," and is the title given to the head of a family in Old Testament times prior to the time of Moses.[6]

---

[6] Smith's Bible Dictionary: Patriarch.

Adam

Circa 4,000 B.C.
Genesis 1–4; 5:1–5; Moses 1–5; 6:1–12; Abraham 4:26–31; 5

Adam was "the first flesh upon the earth, the first man also"—the Patriarch and "father of the human family."[7] He is also known as Michael the Archangel,[8] "the prince of all, the ancient of days"[9] spoken of by Daniel the prophet.[10] He was not born in the traditional sense, but was formed by God from the dust of the earth. Shortly after his creation, the Lord called all the animals and birds together and brought them to Adam to see what he would call them, and he named them all.

The Lord planted a garden "eastward in Eden" and put Adam in it "to dress it, and to keep it." In the midst of the garden, the Lord planted two very special trees: "the tree of life," and "the tree of knowledge of good and evil." The Lord told Adam he could eat freely of every tree in the garden, including the tree of life, but he could not eat from the tree of knowledge of good and evil. However, he was told he could choose for himself.

Later, when God decided that Adam needed a companion, he caused Adam to fall into a deep sleep. While he slept, He took one of Adam's ribs and "closed up the flesh in the stead thereof."

---

[7] History of the Church 3:387.
[8] Jude 1:9; History of the Church 3:386.
[9] Doctrine & Covenants 27:11.
[10] Daniel 7:9; 12:1.

From that rib, God created a woman and brought her to Adam to be a "help meet" and companion. Adam said she was "bone of my bones," and named her Eve. That she was made from one of Adam's ribs can be taken as a symbolic lesson to teach men that women are equal to men and are not to be ruled over or trampled underfoot. Adam also notes that a man should "leave his father and his mother, and shall cleave unto his *wife;* and they shall be one flesh." (Emphasis added.)

Adam and Eve were left innocent in the Garden of Eden for a time and "they were both naked, the man and his wife, and were not ashamed," not knowing good from evil. Had they not been tempted by the devil and succumbed to that temptation they, and all other animal life, would have remained in the Garden forever. But if they had remained in their state of innocence, they "would have had no children."[11]

We don't know how long Adam and Eve lived in the Garden of Eden, but the plan could not continue as long as they remained in this state. So it is logical to assume that they were not there very long before temptation entered their lives.

The story of the fall of Adam is well-known and need not be repeated in detail. Satan came, Eve ate the fruit from the tree of knowledge, then she gave some to Adam; thus, they both sinned (or transgressed, "for sin is the transgression of the law").[12] When the Lord called for Adam, he and Eve hid from Him, as we frequently do (or attempt to do) when we're caught in an act of disobedience. But the Lord knew where they were and would now hold them accountable for their sins. They were frightened, not only because they had done wrong, but also because they knew what their punishment would be—they would "die" because they had eaten the forbidden fruit against God's wishes. When confronted by God, Adam blamed Eve for tempting him to eat the fruit. Eve simply said the devil made her do it. But their excuses

---

[11] 2 Nephi 2:22, 23. [12] 1 John 3:4.

were to no avail, they were both punished. Although Adam and Eve lived a long life upon the earth, eventually physical death came upon them and as a result, upon all men.[13]

But the real death—the one with eternal consequences—came much more rapidly. In the Garden, Adam and Eve had walked in the presence of God the Eternal Father and received his counsel; now, in their fallen state, that privilege would no longer be possible. They were cast out of the Garden and became spiritually dead[14]—separated from God forever until He instructed them in the Plan of Salvation and provided the method by which they could return to His presence.

Expelled from the Garden and with the price of their disobedience and punishment fresh in mind, Adam began a normal human existence. To provide for Eve and himself, he tilled the ground, planted seeds, gathered flocks of animals, and with Eve, began a family. He called upon God, heard His voice, and received His commandments: Adam and his posterity were to worship "the Lord their God," and sacrifice the firstborn of their flocks. Adam obeyed without even knowing why, and so the ordinance of sacrifice began. An angel appeared to Adam one day and asked him why he was sacrificing. Adam answered in the only way he could: "I know not, save the Lord commanded me." The angel then gave this explanation: "This thing is a similitude of the sacrifice of the Only Begotten of the Father, which is full of grace and truth. Wherefore, thou shalt do all that thou doest in the name of the Son, and thou shalt repent and call upon God in the name of the Son forevermore." This, of course, became a universal commandment.

Adam blessed God and began to "prophesy concerning all the families of the earth." He understood the Plan of Salvation, was baptized, and received the Holy Ghost (or the baptism of fire), thus being "born of the Spirit, and . . . quickened in the inner man." That Adam taught his posterity the doctrines of salvation

---

[13] 1 Corinthians 15:22.   [14] Doctrine & Covenants 29:41.

was confirmed by the teachings of Enoch and revealed in the story of our first parents as recorded by Moses.

Adam kept a book of his generations. He ordained Abel to the priesthood,[15] but Abel was killed by Cain. One hundred and thirty years passed before Seth was born, another man after Adam's own image. Adam also ordained Seth (and others) to the priesthood.[16]

Finally, at the age of nine hundred and twenty-seven, Adam called his descendants together at Adam-ondi-Ahman and bestowed upon them his blessing. The Lord appeared to them ". . . and blessed Adam, and called him Michael, the prince, the archangel."[17] At this final patriarchal meeting and as head of the family of all men and the first prophet, Adam predicted what would befall his posterity "unto the latest generation."[18] All of this was written in the Book of Enoch,[19] a record that has been lost. Adam will come again to Adam-ondi-Ahman (originally called Spring Hill, Daviess County, Missouri), to visit his people and sit in judgment as the Ancient of Days, just as Daniel the prophet testified.[20]

Although some parts of the story of Adam and the creation can be thought of as allegorical or parabolic, there is ample evidence in the New Testament that Adam existed, and that the New Testament Church taught and believed in the basic facts and teachings of Adam's story. (Some of these New Testament references are only incidental.)[21] Paul, however, taught the doctrine of the fall and its results: that Adam's sin brought death into the world and that death will come to us all. But because of Christ, that result will not be permanent.[22] Paul testified to the Corinthians that Christ had risen from the dead and continued by saying that, "since by man [Adam] came death, by man [Christ] came also the resurrection of the dead." He concluded that "as in Adam all die,

[15] Doctrine & Covenants 84:16.
[16] Doctrine & Covenants 107:42–50.
[17] Doctrine & Covenants 107:54.
[18] Doctrine & Covenants 107:56.
[19] Doctrine & Covenants 107:57.

[20] History of the Church 3:35, 385–92.
[21] Luke 3:38; Matthew 19:4–6 (referring to Genesis 1:27; 2:24); Jude 1:14.
[22] Romans 5:12–21.

even so in Christ shall all be made alive."[23] Paul confirmed to Timothy that Adam was formed before Eve and was not deceived by the devil, but that Eve *was* deceived. Paul apparently had some problem with women and insinuated that Adam knew the consequences of his choice, yet made it knowingly[24]— as if sinning knowingly was better than being deceived by Satan, which, of course, it is not.

An interesting story of the fall from the Jewish perspective was written by Josephus, a Jewish historian who was born in A.D. 37 and died sometime after A.D. 100. This rendition vividly shows the deviation that had taken place in the story of the creation by that time. Josephus gave the serpent "legs" and an "envious disposition." He had it actually speak with Eve, and when it was finally punished by God, it could no longer speak and its *legs* were removed so that it would slither thereafter rather than walk.[25]

Adam, the first prophet, lived a total of nine hundred and thirty years before he died. (Genesis 5:5.)

[23] 1 Corinthians 15:21, 22.
[24] 1 Timothy 2:14.

[25] Josephus Antiquities Book 1.1.1–4.

Abel

Circa 4,000 B.C.
Genesis 4; Moses 5

Abel was the second son of Adam and Eve. The name "Abel" is not interpreted in the Bible. It has been variously defined as *sorrow* by the Jewish historian Josephus,[26] and as *vanity,*[27] *breath, vapor, and transitoriness* by others[28]—all of which confirms that no one is sure of the name's meaning. Abel was a shepherd. Cain, his older brother, was a tiller of the soil. No records are available of Abel's teachings or ministry; however, Abel is included as a prophet based on the comment by the Lord to the Jews when he held them accountable for "the blood of all the prophets . . . from the blood of Abel unto the blood of Zacharias . . . ."

Abel is only mentioned in the Bible in Genesis, Chapter 4. That chapter records the scant facts of his birth, his sacrifice to the Lord, the anger of his brother Cain toward him, and his murder by Cain, making him the Bible's first martyr. The verses in Genesis 4 point out that Abel's sacrifice was accepted by the Lord while Cain's was rejected—which indicates that Adam taught both Cain and Abel the requirement of sacrifice. After the murder, the Lord asked Cain what had happened to Abel. Cain's memorable response was, "I know not: Am I my brother's keeper?" Of course,

---

[26] Josephus Antiquities 1.2.1.
[27] Catholic Encyclopedia: Abel.

[28] Smith's Bible Dictionary: Abel.

the Lord knew what had occurred and thereafter punished Cain for murdering his brother.

The same story is told in Moses and includes some additional detail. In those verses we learn that Cain married one of his brother's daughters, presumably a daughter of Abel. However, the subject of Cain's marriage has given rise to several legends, one being that Cain and Abel each had a twin sister, whom they were to marry. But Abel's sister was more beautiful than Cain's, and Cain desired her for his wife rather than his own twin sister—thus providing an additional motive for the slaying of his brother.

In the New Testament, John records that Abel was murdered by Cain because Cain's works "were evil, and his brother's righteous."[29] Paul references Abel's sacrifice (of either his own blood or the blood of his offering to the Lord) when he states that the sacrificial blood of Jesus was more efficacious than the sacrifice of Abel.[30]

Because there are no other references to Abel in the scriptures, leaving only legends surrounding him, we're left to wonder even if he was married or had children, (other than the supposition that Cain married one of Abel's daughters as can be inferred from the scripture in Moses).[31] Even his age, the manner in which he was killed, and his burial are left to the imagination. This has also given rise to many legends. Some say Cain struck Abel with a stone, some a cane, and others that he choked him. Abel's burial has also been the subject of some interesting legends. Some of them locate his burial near Hebron and others claim it was by Damascus. Because this was assumed to be the first human burial on earth, writers have unwittingly denied Adam the intelligence to properly dispose of the body. Jewish tradition has it that Abel's dog stood by his body to fend off the beasts of prey until two turtle doves landed close to Adam (or perhaps some of his family members) and one of the birds died. The remaining dove scratched

---

[29] 1 John 3:12.
[30] Hebrews 11:4; 12:24.
[31] Moses 5:28.

Prophets of the Old Testament

out a small hole in the soil and moved the dead bird into it. Supposedly, this is how Adam learned the proper way to bury Abel. The Koran identifies the helpful bird as a crow who instructs Cain so that he can hide his shame.[32] Much of the tradition and legend surrounding Abel has been left to supposition because the scriptural record only mentions that "Cain rose up against Abel his brother, and slew him."

---

[32] Jewish Encyclopedia: Abel; Koran: sura v. 30 et seq.

Enoch

3443–3013 B.C.

Genesis 5:18–24; Moses 5–6

Enoch is thought to have lived between 3443–3013 B.C. His name in Hebrew means *initiate* or *initiator.* Enoch is involved in only seven verses in the Old Testament text, one of which is the linage recitation in Genesis 5:18. He was sixty-five at the birth of his son Methuselah, and he "walked with God," an indication of the high level of his righteousness. He lived a total of three hundred and sixty-five years. Of his demise the verses say, "And Enoch walked with God: and he was not; for God took him." Paul's explanation of Enoch's "taking" is that Enoch was "translated that he should not see death; and was not found, because God had translated him: for before his translation he had this testimony, that he pleased God."[33]

Jude verifies that some of Enoch's writings were available to him when he quoted one of Enoch's prophecies: "Behold, the Lord cometh with ten thousands of his saints, [t]o execute judgment upon all, and to convince all that are ungodly among them of all their ungodly deeds which they have . . . committed, and of all their hard speeches which ungodly sinners have spoken against him."[34] The only other Biblical mention of Enoch is in Luke's genealogical lineage of Jesus' stepfather, Joseph.[35]

[33] Hebrews 11:5.
[34] Jude 1:14, 15.
[35] Luke 3:37.

From latter day revelation, we learn that Enoch was ordained by Adam when he was twenty-five, blessed by Adam at sixty-five, saw the Lord and walked with Him continually, was four hundred and thirty years old when he was translated (rather than three hundred and sixty-five per the Bible), and that somewhere there is a Book of Enoch.[36] In fact, there are three apocalyptic books that claim to be the Book of Enoch. But an authentic Book of Enoch has yet to be revealed or confirmed.[37]

However, additional information about Enoch is available in the Book of Moses. It tells us that Enoch was called by the Lord to be a prophet and instructed to call the people to repentance when he was sixty-five years old. Enoch's response to the call was to bow himself to the ground and put forth three reasons why he was not eligible for this call: (1) he was too young, (2) the people hated him, and (3) he had some kind of speech problem. But the Lord wanted Enoch to be his prophet, so He answered the three objections as follows: (1) just do it, (2) no one will harm you, and (3) leave the "slow[ness] of speech" problem up to Me. Then the Lord gave Enoch this phenomenal blessing: "Behold my Spirit is upon you, wherefore all thy words will I justify; and the mountains shall flee before you, and the rivers shall turn from their course; and thou shalt abide in me, and I in you; therefore walk with me."

Immediately thereafter, the Lord commanded Enoch to anoint his eyes with clay, which he did. He then beheld a great vision of the spirits God had created and as a result, the word went abroad that "A seer hath the Lord raised up unto his people." But his preaching didn't produce universal repentance. At first, "all men

[36] Doctrine & Covenants 107:48–49, 57.
[37] There are many sources, printings, and references describing and commenting on the writings of Enoch. For detail concerning the three sources of the book of Enoch, the text of the Book of Enoch, and some of the legends surrounding Enoch's life, city, ministry, and writings, see: Milik, Jazef. T., ed. "The Books of Enoch: Aramaic Fragments of Qumran Cave 4

(Oxford, 1976). These, as well as many books of like subject, are called pseudepigrapha writings, meaning they claim to be written by a biblical character, but their scriptural authenticity has been and still remains questioned. Because of this questioned authenticity, the Book of Enoch was not included in any of the Jewish or Christian Old Testament Canons.

were offended because of him" and said that "a wild man hath come among us." Consequently, the people sent an emissary to Enoch. "Tell us plainly," the emissary said. "Who thou art, and from whence thou comest?" Enoch then testified of his origin and call. This revelation frightened the people and they "trembled, and could not stand in his presence."

Enoch continued his ministry and taught of Jesus Christ and the requirements for gaining the kingdom. He talked with the Lord "face to face," and his faith and the power of his language were so great that at his command mountains fled, rivers turned out of their courses, the roar of lions was heard, and "all nations feared greatly."

Those who did believe in Enoch were called "Zion" because they were of "one heart and one mind, and dwelt in righteousness; and there was no poor among them." Enoch built a city for those who repented and followed him. He called it "the City of Holiness, even ZION." This city—and Enoch—were eventually taken up into heaven. Thereafter, Enoch received his vision of "all the nations of the earth," and all that would happen to them, including Noah and the great flood brought on by the persistent wickedness of all humankind. He foresaw the first coming of Jesus, His crucifixion, the establishment of the New Jerusalem, the last days, all things leading to the end of the world, and the Savior's millennial reign.

Indeed, a great seer had come among the people. The hearts of some men and women were filled with righteousness. A sacred place of refuge, called Zion, was established, and "Enoch and his people walked with God, and he dwelt in the midst of Zion; and it came to pass that Zion was not, for God received it up into his own bosom; and from thence went forth the saying, ZION IS FLED."

. . .

Noah

2948–1998 B.C.
Genesis 6:8–22; 7–9; Moses 7:42, 43; 8:12–30

T he great prophet Noah was tenth in the "line" from Seth, the son of Adam. His name is translated as *rest,* and his spiritual name is *Gabriel.*[38] From records of the restoration, we learn that Noah was ordained by Methuselah into the priesthood when he was ten years old.[39]

Other than the main story of Noah found in Genesis and Moses, references to him are used by scriptural writers in many ways. Paul testified that it was because of Noah's faith that he was saved from the flood,[40] while Ezekiel said Noah and his family were saved because of their righteousness.[41] The Lord Himself used the story of the flood to describe the wickedness that would prevail over the earth just prior to the Second Coming[42] and to confirm that He fulfills His promises.[43]

Noah's name is spelled Noe in Luke's New Testament genealogical linage.[44] The Book of Mormon prophet Ether used the story of the flood to verify that the Western Hemisphere is also a promised land.[45] But the most enlightening information comes from Peter. He tells us that those who were destroyed by the flood

---

38 History of the Church 3:386.
39 Doctrine & Covenants 107:52.
40 Hebrews 11:7.
41 Ezekiel 14:14, 20.

42 Matthew 24:37, 38; Luke 17:26, 27.
43 Isaiah 54:9.
44 Luke 3:36.
45 Ether 13:2.

were cast into a spiritual prison until some future day of potential redemption when the gospel would be preached to them as a result of the Savior's ministry to the spirit world.[46]

Noah's introduction in the Old Testament indicates that he lived five hundred years and then "begat Shem, Ham, and Japheth." In the book of Moses, he is introduced in the vision of Enoch when Enoch saw all of the future nations of the earth. Noah's birth was also prophesied in the book of Moses by Methuselah and the order of Noah's children is recorded there as: Jepheth, born when Noah was four hundred and fifty years old; Shem, born forty-two years later; and Ham, born eight years after Shem. Thereafter, it was declared that Noah's sons "hearkened unto the Lord, and gave heed, and they were called the sons of God." It was said of Noah that he was a perfect man in his generation and both he and his sons found "grace in the eyes of the Lord." Noah taught the things of God, as the prophets before him had done. While Enoch saw that Noah built an ark and that the Lord smiled upon it, the rest of the story is found in Genesis.

Both Genesis and Moses agree that the wickedness of men and women became so great in the days of Noah "that every imagination of the thoughts of [their] heart[s] was only evil continually," a most deplorable condition. And so, it "repented Noah [not the Lord] . . . that the Lord had made man on the earth." Just how long did Noah preach while the ark was being constructed? The answer comes from a combination of scriptures. Peter declares that "the long suffering of God *waited* in the days of Noah, while the ark was a preparing."[47] In Genesis, the Lord reduced the longevity of man from the centuries-long ages of the Patriarchs to only one hundred and twenty years. Combining the two, it would indicate that Noah preached for one hundred and twenty years while building the ark, which gave time for the children of men to repent of their wickedness before they would be destroyed in the prophesied deluge.

[46] 1 Peter 3:18–20.

[47] 1 Peter 3:20 emphasis added.

But no amount of sermonizing could cure the evils of human-kind, and the time finally came when the earth was totally corrupt and filled with violence. (This apparently included some of the daughters of Noah's sons.) The Lord told Noah that "the end of all flesh is come before me . . . and, behold, I will destroy them . . . ." The Lord gave Noah the design and dimensions for the ark and specified that it be built of gopher wood. He also promised that He would establish His covenant with Noah, and Noah did "according to all that God commanded him."

How big was the ark? The scripture declares it to be 300 cubits long, 50 cubits broad, and 30 cubits high. Estimating a cubit at the customary 22.5 inches, the boat would have measured 562.5 feet long, 93.67 feet wide, and 56.25 feet deep. Historically, there have been numerous estimates of the ark's size ranging from the above to the absurd dimensions given by Origen in order to confuse Celsus. Origen's measurements made the ark twenty-five miles long and three-quarters of a mile wide![48]

Noah was commanded to preserve animal life upon the earth and finally warned that in seven days the flood was to come. He took pairs of both clean and unclean beasts and fowls into the ark as he was commanded, and in the six hundredth year of Noah's life, the Lord broke up the "fountains of the great deep," opened the "windows of heaven," and shut Noah and his family into the ark. Then it rained for forty days and forty nights. Soon, water covered the whole earth by a depth of fifteen cubits. The water destroyed all flesh that was upon the land, and "prevailed upon the earth an hundred and fifty days." When the waters finally receded, the ark came to rest on the "mountains of Ararat," a general description that does *not* identify the specific (and much sought after) mountain called "Ararat."

Noah and his family remained in the ark for some time after he landed. He sent out a raven to see if there was any dry land,

48 International Standard Bible Encyclopedia: Ark of Noah.

but it returned. Then he released a dove, but it also returned. Finally, after another seven days, Noah released a second dove and it returned carrying an olive leaf. From that sign, Noah concluded that the flood was receding. After an additional seven days a third dove was released, but it did not return. Noah thereupon left the ark with all his company. His first priority was to build an altar and give thanks to the Lord, and the Lord commanded him to multiply and replenish the earth, just as He had Adam and Eve. After Noah completed his sacrifice the animals were released and the natural animosity between man and beast that had been dormant on the ark was reestablished.

All evil had been destroyed from off the earth, and the great flood had abated. Then the Lord made a covenant with Noah and his generations that all flesh would never again be destroyed by a flood. As a sign of that covenant, the Lord "set [His] bow in the cloud" —the rainbow—as a sign or token of the covenant.

The only other specific story about Noah in the scriptures notes that he planted vineyards, produced wine, and became drunken from it. He lay "uncovered within his tent" and Ham saw his "nakedness." Ham reported the potentially embarrassing situation to his brothers. They backed into the tent and covered Noah with a blanket before he awoke. Although no additional information is given about what happened when Ham discovered Noah uncovered, Noah cursed Ham for his action when he blessed his three sons.

The blessings are the last we hear from this important prophet. Noah stated, "blessed be the Lord God of Shem," which would indicate that although Shem was the second son, he received the birthright blessing. This may be the reason why Shem is the first listed in the Biblical account. Japheth was promised that he would be enlarged, but that he would dwell in tents. The curse laid on Ham was that he, with the people of Canaan who descended from him, would be a servant to Shem.

Noah was nine hundred and fifty years of age when he died.

Abraham

1996–1822 B.C.
Genesis 11:26– 25:18; Abraham 1–3

Abraham's name means *father of a multitude*. He was first called
Abram, which meant *exalted father*. Later, the Lord changed
his name to Abraham, which will be used throughout the following text.

The story of Abraham is told in many places,[49] perhaps because he is considered the father of the Hebrew nation and many
other civilizations. His influence has framed the basic beliefs of
Judaism, Christianity, and Islam. Through his wives—Sarah,
Hagar, and Keturah—his descendants have populated a multitude of nations. Isaac (his second son considered by the Bible to
be the only legitimate son) was born to Sarah, whom the Jews
consider his sole legitimate wife. Ishmael, who is the progenitor
of the Arab nations, was Abraham's first son by the concubine
Hagar, Sarah's handmaiden. After the expulsion of Hagar and the
death of Sarah, Abraham took Keturah to wife and she bore him
six sons, Zimran, Jokshan, Medan, Midian, Ishbok, and Shuah.
The descendants of the sons of Keturah became the ancestors of

[49] Smith's Bible Dictionary: Abraham; Josephus
Antiquities 1.7–17; The Catholic Encyclopedia:
Abraham; Wikepedia Encyclopedia: Abraham;
International Standard Bible Encyclopedia:
Abraham; The Torah: A Modern Commentary
pp. 87–169.

the nomadic tribes inhabiting the countries south and southeast of Palestine.[50]

The story of Abraham begins with his birth, along with that of his brothers, Nehor and Haran. They lived with their father, Terah, in Ur of the Chaldees. Although in biblical geography there are two cities named Ur, one in northern Syria and one near the mouth of the Euphrates, it is the latter that is deemed by many to be the area where Abraham and his family originally lived.

Haran, Abraham's brother, died in Ur and was buried there. Although we're not told the name of Haran's wife, we are given the names of at least three of his children: Lot, Saria, and Milcah. It was in Ur that Abraham and Nehor took themselves wives: Abraham married Sarai (hereafter Sarah) and Nehor married Milcah, both daughters of Haran and nieces to their husbands.

It was about this time that Abraham determined he should depart from his father's homeland. He announced that he was a "follower of righteousness" and desired to acquire "great knowledge," and to be a "father of many nations." And so he "sought . . . appointment unto the Priesthood according to the appointment of God" and was ordained "a High Priest, holding the right belonging to the fathers." However, before he left Ur, the priests of Pharaoh attempted to sacrifice Abraham upon an altar to their gods (but he was saved by Jehovah). He also affirmed that he had received the former patriarchs' records concerning the right to the Priesthood. Those records included "a knowledge of the beginning of the creation, and also of the planets, and of the stars, as they were made known unto the fathers." That Abraham had this knowledge of the celestial heavens was also confirmed by Josephus when he related the traditional teachings of the Jews regarding this prophet.[51] Soon after these experiences, Abraham left Ur.

After leaving Ur, many unique things happened to Abraham. For example, because of Sarah's beauty, he twice feared for his own life. To protect himself, he had Sarah claim she was his sister rather

[50] Smith's Bible Dictionary: Abraham.   [51] Josephus Antiquities 1.7.1, 2.

than his wife. Many years later at ninety-nine, he "fell upon his face, and laughed" when an angel told him that Sarah would yet bear a child. Sarah also laughed when she overheard the same promise. It was during this encounter that Abram's name was changed to Abraham, and Saria's to Sarah. Finally, what became known as the Abrahamic Covenant[52] was completed between the Lord and Abraham and the "token" or sign of the covenant—circumcision—was given.

From Abraham, the covenant passed first to Isaac and then to Jacob, whose name was changed to Israel. The covenant then went to the twelve sons of Jacob, collectively known as the twelve tribes (or house) of Israel. When the children of Israel sinned, the blessings of the Abrahamic covenant were withdrawn from them, but the covenant remained.

Another story about Abraham relates how he bartered with Jehovah over the sin-filled cities of Sodom and Gomorrah. The Lord told Abraham he was about to destroy those cities because of their wickedness, but Lot, Abraham's nephew, was living there and Abraham did not want him destroyed. The basis for the bargaining was thus established. Abraham asked if the Lord would destroy the city if fifty righteous people were to be found therein. The Lord said no, they wouldn't be destroyed. But Abraham, knowing that fifty righteous could not be found, bartered the number down to forty, then thirty, then twenty, and finally ten. But there weren't even as few as ten righteous people in Sodom! Two angels were dispatched for a final verification of the number of righteous-souled people left in the city. They visited Lot and told him that if he wanted to save himself, he must leave the city with his family. Lot, his wife, and two unmarried daughters left, even though he could not convince the sons-in-law married to his other daughters to leave. It is presumed that they were destroyed with the city. On the road out of town, Lot's wife, in defiance of the Lord's warning not to look back, turned to watch the destruction. The scriptures

[52] The Second Coming of Jesus the Messiah, p. 23.

indicate she was turned into a "pillar of salt" because of her disobedience.

Perhaps the most unique experience Abraham had was when the Lord commanded him to make a sacrifice of his son, Isaac. Abraham was obedient and Isaac innocently compliant. They proceeded to the place of sacrifice where Abraham "bound Isaac his son, and laid him on the altar upon the wood. And Abraham stretched forth his hand and took the knife to slay his son." But the angel of the Lord stopped Abraham and praised him for not withholding his only son from the Lord. This episode is regarded as a similitude of the future sacrifice of the Son of God by the Eternal Father.

Abraham had great visions, including that of the "intelligences that were organized before the world was." He acquired knowledge of those souls who were "noble and great" (including himself), envisioned the Savior accepting His great calling, and witnessed the presentation of the Plan of Salvation. Those who accepted the Plan moved on to their "second estate," while those who rebelled and refused to accept the Father's Plan were cast out. After that, Abraham was privileged to record the creation of the earth and all thereon, having spoken with the Lord "face to face." The Lord also told Abraham about the four-hundred-year enslavement of the Israelites that would occur in the future.

Sarah died before Abraham, and after some bartering, land was purchased for her burial site in "the cave of the field of Machpelah before Mamre: the same is Hebron in the land of Canaan."

Later, Abraham arranged the marriage of Isaac by directing his servant to go to his brother Nehor, who lived in Mesopotamia, to find a wife. After requesting a sign from the Lord, the servant was successful in his search and returned with Rebekah, daughter of Nehor (and Abraham's niece) for Isaac to marry. Thereafter, Abraham married Keturah in his old age, and she bore him six sons. At the time of his death, he only gave gifts to his "concubines," and "gave all that he had unto Isaac."

There are many references to Abraham in the New Testament, the Book of Mormon, and the Doctrine & Covenants that provide a wealth of information—all of which at one time or another (when speaking of the origin of God's dealings with the covenant people) refer to the God of Abraham, Isaac, and Jacob. He is accounted as the father of the faithful and of the covenant people.

During His ministry, the Lord occasionally included references to Abraham in His teaching, using "Abraham's bosom" in the parable of Lazarus and the rich man as the recognized destination of the righteous after this life when they die.[53] And He enraged the Jewish leadership when He witnessed His divinity to them by declaring, "Before Abraham was, I am."[54]

Two significant elements of Abraham's existence are revealed in modern revelation. First, he was chosen before he was born to be a leader in the kingdom of God; and second, because of his righteous obedience, he has been exalted and sits upon a throne in eternity.[55]

Abraham lived one hundred and seventy-five years before he died and was buried beside his beloved Sarah in the cave at Machpelah. No information is given as to the death or burial places of Hagar or Keturah.

---

[53] Luke 16:19–31.
[54] John 8:58.

[55] Doctrine & Covenants 132:29, 37.

Isaac

1897–1717 B.C.
Genesis 24; 25:19–34; 26–28:1

Even though Isaac lived one hundred and eighty years, only fleeting glimpses of his life are recorded in the Old Testament record, and little more than that in the records of the restoration.

Isaac's name means *laughter* or *he laugheth*, presumably because of the laughter of both Abraham and Sarah at the announcement that they would give birth to a son in their old age. Sarah was ninety and Abraham one hundred when Isaac was born. Interestingly, from this story comes the modern legal term, "fertile octogenarian," meaning that the law presumes a woman is never too old to give birth.

Isaac was the birthright son (even though he wasn't the first son born to Abraham), and the Lord promised Abraham that He would "establish [His] covenant with him for an everlasting covenant and with his seed after him," ensuring the continuation of the Abrahamic Covenant.

The first recorded incident after Isaac's birth is the rivalry between Isaac and his older brother Ishmael, the son of Hagar, Sarah's Egyptian handmaiden. Sarah caught Ishmael "mocking" Isaac and asked Abraham to "Cast out this bondwoman and her son: for the son of this bondwoman shall not be heir with my son, even with Isaac"[56] (even though Sarah had given Hagar to Abraham so that Abraham would have a descendant). Abraham was grieved because of Sarah's ultimatum, but the Lord assured him that He would take care of Hagar and Ishmael and that Abraham should do as Sarah requested.

The next incident involves the Lord's commandment for Abraham to offer Isaac as a sacrifice. The story is told in some detail, with Isaac's only concern being that his father had not thought to bring an offering to be used upon the altar. Abraham assured Isaac that the Lord would provide. The story has always been seen as a similitude of God offering his Only Begotten Son for the sins of the world.[57]

Isaac was forty years old when he married. The story of how he acquired a wife is unique. Abraham did not want his son to take a wife from among the Canaanites, in whose land they dwelled, so he sent one of his servants to the city of his brother, Nehor, to find Isaac a wife. The servant stopped at a well where the daughters of the city came for water and rested himself and his camels. He prayed to the Lord to show him who Isaac's future wife should be by means of a special request: he would ask a woman to provide him with a drink and she would respond that she would provide not only a drink for him, but water for his camels as well. It was Rebekah who fulfilled this scenario in answer to the servant's prayers. After consulting with her father and brother, she willingly accompanied the servant back to Abraham's home where she became Isaac's wife.

Later, a famine struck Canaan and the Lord appeared to Isaac and told him not to go into Egypt but to stay in the land of Gerar, ruled by Abimelech, king of the Philistines. But Abimelech had eyes for Rebekah, so to preserve his life, Isaac tells Abimelech that Rebekah is his sister, not his wife, a circumstance similar to that of Abraham and Sarah in Egypt. But owing to Abimelech's desire to have Rebekah and the Philistines' envy of Isaac's wealth, Isaac is disposed to leave the area. It is at this point that the Lord appears to Isaac and confirms the Covenant of Abraham upon him.

---

[56] Genesis 21:9, 10.   [57] Genesis 22:1–14.

Rebekah eventually produces twin sons, Esau and Jacob. With Jacob grasping his heel, Esau was the firstborn. He was hairy and red in physical appearance, while Jacob was smooth. Before the twins were born, however, the Lord told Rebekah that the elder of them would serve the younger, a prophecy that was fulfilled when Esau sold his birthright to Jacob for a bowl of pottage, and was sealed with the patriarchal blessing Isaac gave his two sons.

As Isaac grew old, his eyesight dimmed and he was aware that his days were numbered. He wanted to give his sons their patriarchal blessings and in preparation for the event, he asked Esau to bring him the "savoury meat" that he loved for dinner. While Esau was off on his deer hunt, Rebekah, using Esau's recipe, substituted "two kids of the goats" in the stead thereof, and had Jacob disguise himself in Esau's clothing so he could take it to Isaac. She even had Jacob place the skins of the kids on his "hands, and upon the smooth of his neck" so that Isaac would think he was Esau. Jacob did all that his mother told him to do and pretending to be Esau, he successfully deceived Isaac and received the birthright blessing that he had purchased from Esau. Esau later married one of the daughters of Canaan against his father's wishes while Jacob selected a wife from Isaac's kin. This famous story will be recounted in more detail in the chapter on the prophet Jacob.

Although little is recorded of Isaac's life, his greatness may be assumed because he was blessed to see God twice. It appears that the chroniclers of the Old Testament used him as a bridge between Abraham and Jacob by telling bits and pieces of his story, thereby ensuring that the reader knows the Covenant continued through him from Abraham to Jacob. From the scriptures of the restoration, we learn that he was exalted and sits on an eternal throne, having done that which the Lord commanded him to do.[58]

"And the days of Isaac were an hundred and fourscore years. And Isaac gave up the ghost, and died, and was gathered unto his people, being old and full of days."[59]

---

[58] Doctrine & Covenants 132:37.   [59] Genesis 35:27–29.

Prophets of the Old Testament

Jacob

1837–1691 B.C.
Genesis 27–35; 49

The most memorable story about Jacob is that of his genuine love for Rachel. He bargained with Laban, her father, that he would labor seven years for the privilege of her hand in marriage, only to be deceived by his father-in-law and have the "tender eyed" Leah, Rachel's older sister, placed in his darkened tent where he took her to wife. However, after agreeing to labor another seven years for his father-in-law, and waiting a week to honor the marriage with Leah, he was given the lovely Rachel as his wife. Thus Jacob labored a total of fourteen years for the wife he desired.

Jacob, whose name means *supplanter,* was a twin, born second to Esau. For twenty years of marriage to Isaac, Rebekah was unable to bear children. Then the Lord blessed her with the twins. Other than the birth, where Esau was born with Jacob holding onto his heel, we know little of the early life of the two brothers. Two verses of scripture tell us, "And the boys grew: and Esau was a cunning hunter, a man of the field; and Jacob was a plain man, dwelling in tents. And Isaac loved Esau, because he did eat of his venison: but Rebekah loved Jacob."

On one occasion, Esau returned from an unsuccessful hunting trip and "was faint." He asked Jacob to give him some "red pottage" to eat because he felt he was at the "point to die." Jacob agreed to feed Esau, but only if he would sell him his birthright for the food. Because Esau had been born first and was the oldest, he was the birthright son. However, during her pregnancy the Lord had told Rebekah that the older son would serve the younger, and that the descendants of the younger son would be stronger than those of the elder. Thus, when Esau sold his birthright to Jacob, the Lord's prophecy (given before his birth) was fulfilled. But the full realization of the blessing was yet to come, and it came as the result of a story of deception instigated by Rebekah, who was determined to ensure the birthright blessing for Jacob.

Isaac was old and "his eyes were dim," meaning that he was almost blind. He felt that his death was near and therefore requested that Esau go into the field, bring back some venison and prepare the "savoury meat" that he loved, after which he would give him his blessing. Rebekah overheard the conversation and told Jacob to retrieve two "kids of the goats" and she would prepare them as "savoury meat" for Isaac. Jacob was then to take the meat to Isaac, pretend to be Esau, and receive the blessing. But Jacob questioned his mother's plan because, he noted, in spite of Isaac's poor eyesight, "Esau my brother is a hairy man, and I am a smooth man." If Isaac were to reach out and touch Jacob, the deception would fail and Isaac would curse Jacob rather than bless him. To solve the problem, Rebekah told Jacob that if the plan didn't work out, she would accept the curse herself.

Rebekah prepared the food and to enhance the deception, dressed Jacob in Esau's clothes so that the smell of Esau would be on him. She than put the "skins of the kids of the goats upon his hands, and upon the smooth of his neck" to camouflage Jacob's smoothness, and sent him into Isaac's tent. The deception worked (even though the thought runs through the mind that Isaac could surely tell the difference between the hair on a man's arms and neck from that of a goat and was not really deceived) and he gave the birthright blessing to Jacob just as God foretold. When Esau returned, prepared the venison, and entered Isaac's tent, he found that his brother had deceptively taken away his blessing. Esau was angry. He hated Jacob and planned to kill him. But Rebekah again interfered and with Isaac's blessing, sent Jacob away to her brother Laban. Before he goes Isaac again blesses Jacob with the blessings of Abraham, thus completing the birthright blessing by granting Jacob the covenant established between God and Abraham. This fact perhaps confirms the assumption that even though Isaac's eyes were dim, his fingers were not insensitive, and he knew all along who was ordained to receive the birthright blessing.

While on his way to Laban's house in Padanaram, Jacob had the dream known as "Jacob's ladder," a dream of angels climbing up and down on a ladder between heaven and earth. Jacob saw God at the top of the ladder, and He confirmed the blessings of the covenant of Abraham that Isaac had given Jacob. When he awoke, Jacob recognized the holiness of his surroundings. He took the stones he had used as pillows for his sleep and made a pillar. He poured oil on it and named the site Bethel, meaning *the house of God*. Jacob then bargained with God: if God would bless him with safety, food, clothing, and peace, he would give Him a tithe— a tenth of all.

Jacob's story now turns to his love for Rachel. As mentioned before, Jacob and Laban initially agreed that Jacob would work for Laban seven years so that he could have Rachel for his wife. The seven years passed, "and they seemed unto him but a few days, for the love he had to her." After Laban's deception—giving Leah to Jacob instead of Rachel—Jacob honored Leah for a week, then Laban gave him Rachel to wed with the understanding that Jacob would serve him another seven years to pay for her. The scripture notes that "the Lord saw that Leah was hated," and that Jacob loved Rachel "more than Leah," and so he blessed Leah with children and kept Rachel barren. The family story now evolves around that fact.

By the time Leah has four sons Rachel is still barren. She asked Jacob to give her children, but he became angry and declared; "Am I in God's stead?" So Rachel gave Jacob her handmaiden, Bilhah, as her substitute, so that the children of Bilhah would become the children of Rachel. Bilhah becomes the third wife of Jacob and bears two more sons. Leah, not to be outdone by Rachel, gave Zilpah, her handmaiden, to Jacob as his fourth wife. Zilpah also had two sons and thereafter Leah declared, "Happy am I, for the daughters will call me blessed." But the contest between Rachel and Leah did not end there. Leah's firstborn, Reuben, found some mandrake in a field during the wheat harvest. Mandrake is a plant with dark green leaves and purple flowers. Its fruit, when ripe, is about the size of a small apple, ruddy or yellow in color, with both an agreeable smell and taste. The fruit was prized and used as an aphrodisiac. Finding the mandrake was good fortune and Reuben brought it home to his mother, who had stopped having children after the birth of her fourth son, Judah.

When Rachel learned that Leah had the plants, she became upset and asked Leah for some of them, undoubtedly hoping they would cure her barrenness. Leah's response gives insight into the relationship between the two sister-wives. "Is it a small matter that thou hast taken my husband? and wouldest thou take away my son's mandrakes also?" But Rachel knew that Jacob would stay with Leah that night because of the mandrakes, and so responded. Whether Leah gave some of the mandrakes to Rachel, or whether Rachel received them as a bargain for Jacob to stay with Leah, we are not told; but when Jacob returned home from the fields he stayed with Leah when she declared that she had "hired" him because of her son's mandrakes. The result was that Leah eventually produced two more sons and finally, a daughter they named Dinah. And then "God remembered Rachel," and she bore her first son, Joseph.

Jacob now has eleven sons and one daughter by four wives and desires to leave Laban's employ and return to the land promised him by God. He tells Laban to, "Send me away, that I may go unto mine own . . . country. Give me my wives and my children, for whom I have served thee . . . for thou knowest my service which I have done thee." Laban wants him to stay because he has prospered greatly while Jacob has worked for him. However, he reluctantly agrees and instructs Jacob to determine what his wages should be. Jacob replies, "Thou shalt not give me anything: if thou wilt do this thing for me, I will again feed and keep thy flock: I will pass through all thy flock to day, removing from thence all the speckled and spotted cattle, and all the brown cattle among the sheep, and the spotted and speckled among the goats." Jacob said he would take these undesirable animals as his "hire" (or wages) for continuing to work for Laban until he returned to his own land. Laban readily agreed and had his sons remove the specified animals and take them three days journey away from his animals so that they could not crossbreed. Jacob continued to tend Laban's flocks and recovered all the marked animals as additional wages for his labors.

Although God had told Jacob that he would bless him in his efforts, Jacob seemed determined to help things along with his own devices. While he tended Laban's flocks, he used three artifices to increase his own herds and flocks. He took peeled rods or sticks from three trees and placed them in the troughs where the sheep and cattle would drink during breeding season. The offspring became "ringstraked, speckled, and spotted." These he took while young and placed them so that Laban's herds could see them when they conceived, and the young of these animals were also "ringstraked, speckled, and spotted." Finally, he put the rods in the gutters "before the eyes of the cattle" that were the strongest so their offspring would also become those of his herds. All this was done so that Jacob would receive the strongest and Laban the weakest of the herds. It is doubtful whether any of these artifices influenced the type of animal that was conceived, but God continued to bless Jacob and he increased "exceedingly." Laban and his family complained as Jacob prospered, even though Laban changed Jacob's wages ten times during his servitude. Still Jacob's herds and flocks continued to increase.

Jacob then had another dream in which God reminded him of the vow he had made with Him at Bethel, and told him to leave the house of Laban and return to his own land. Following that admonition, Jacob took all that he had and left . . . without even saying goodbye. Laban followed and accused Jacob of not only leaving by stealth, but of stealing his "gods" in the process. Unaware that Rachel had the gods, Jacob told Laban to search the camp, which he does—without success. Eventually the two men establish a truce between them and Jacob continued his journey homeward.

Jacob had been gone for twenty years and as he neared Canaan, old fears arose that Esau still hated him and will do him harm. In anticipation of their meeting, and to placate Esau's feelings, Jacob sent messengers and presents to Esau as he entered Canaan. He separated himself from his company and his herds so that he was alone. During this period, he wrestled all night with "a man." At the break of day, Jacob found that he had been wrestling with an angel who now wanted to leave; but Jacob won't let him go until the angel blessed him. The blessing that followed was common with Old Testament patriarchs. The angel changed Jacob's name. He would no longer be called Jacob, but Israel. Jacob called the name of the place "Peniel: for I have seen God face to face, and my life is preserved."

Esau and Jacob finally reunite in friendship. Esau refuses the gifts Jacob had proffered and they go their separate ways. Shortly after Jacob settles in Canaan, he encounters the first of the problems he will experience with the inhabitants of the land. Simeon and Levi, brothers of Dinah, destroy all the males of Shechem because one of them defiled their sister and Jacob was "troubled" and declared that they would make him a "stink among the inhabitants of the land." God again reveals Himself to Jacob and commands him to go to Bethel and live there. He is also commanded to "make there an altar unto God." Jacob does all this and God appears to him again to confirm that his name will now be Israel (a name that means *the prince that prevails with God*), and confers upon him the blessings and covenants He had made with Abraham and Isaac. During this time Rachel bore Benjamin, the last of Jacob's twelve sons. Although Rachel died during child-birth, the house of Israel is finally established.

Joseph
1746–1636 B.C.
Genesis 37, 39–50; 2 Nephi 3:4–21

T he last fourteen chapters of Genesis (with the exception of Chapter 38, the story of Tamar) tell the story of Joseph, the last of the Prophet-Patriarchs. He was the eleventh-born son of Jacob (whose name was changed to Israel). (Joseph's father is always identified herein by the name Jacob, even though the scriptures use both Jacob and Israel interchangeably.) Joseph was the firstborn son of Rebekah, Jacob's favorite wife. The name "Joseph" means *may God add,* or *may God increase.*[60]

Although Joseph's story has a familiar ring to it, there is no independent evidence available to verify its authenticity. Neither the names of the Pharaoh Joseph served, the Pharaohs during the enslavement, nor the Pharaoh of the Exodus are given—"Pharaoh" being a title, and not a name.[61]

Joseph was seventeen years old at the inception of his story and a "favored" son because his father, Jacob, " loved Joseph more than all his children" and "made him a coat of many colours." As a result, sibling rivalry played a major role in Joseph's early life. The coat of many colors fanned his brothers' envy as a constant visual reminder "that their father loved [Joseph] more than all his breth-

---

[60] Catholic Encyclopedia: Joseph; Smith's Bible [61] The Torah: A Modern Commentary, p. 255. Dictionary: Joseph

ren." As the rivalry intensified, the author of Genesis states that the brothers "hated him, and could not speak peaceably unto him."

To add to the increasing animosity, Joseph had dreams—dreams that he interpreted to his brothers' detriment. The first dream was about sheaves in a field. Joseph's sheaf rose up and those of his brothers bowed down to it. His second dream evidenced an even greater degree of submission and included his parents; in this dream "the sun and the moon and the eleven stars made obeisance to [Joseph]," which brought criticism from Jacob, his father.

The story of the brothers' animosity completes the thirty-seventh chapter of Genesis and begins what has always been referred to as a similitude of the future life of Christ as it was mirrored in Joseph's life. Joseph's brothers plotted to kill him (just as the leadership of the Jews conspired to kill Jesus). They captured him and placed him in a pit. Judah, the eldest brother, saw a caravan of "Ishmeelites" passing by carrying trade goods to Egypt, and he convinced the brothers that instead of killing Joseph, they could sell him for a profit. Thus, for twenty pieces of silver Joseph was sold to the "Ishmeelites" (again a similitude of Judas' sale of Jesus to the leadership of the Jews for thirty pieces of silver).

Joseph is taken to Egypt and sold to Potiphar, the captain of Pharaoh's guard. Some confusion arises here when the author of Genesis describes Joseph's sale. Simply stated: Joseph is *sold to Ishmeelites* by his brothers, but *bought from Midianites* by Potiphar. Because the scriptures report that a caravan of Midianites passed by just before the transaction took place, perhaps the Ishmeelites sold Joseph to the Midianites, who then sold him to Potiphar.

Joseph rose from slavery to become the head of Potiphar's household. He controlled all that Potiphar had, "save the bread which he did eat." It is here that the general theme governing Joseph's life is established. Although Joseph was a "goodly person, and well favoured" and undoubtedly gifted in many ways, his personal leadership capabilities were overshadowed because the scriptures reveal that "the Lord was with Joseph." It was the Lord who was guiding Joseph's destiny.

Joseph's personal integrity and character—his worthiness to be constantly guided by the Lord—is tested when he is tempted by the wife of Potiphar. This scenario (although not the specific temptation) is another similitude of the temptations Jesus encountered from the Jewish leaders and the devil. Like Jesus, Joseph refused to sin under any circumstances. But Potiphar's wife continued her campaign "day by day," with no success. Finally, when they were alone "she caught him by his garment." Joseph escaped her grasp by leaving his garment in her hand. Scorned by his refusals, she falsified and exaggerated the circumstances of the encounter to Potiphar—which caused Potiphar to imprison Joseph— just as false witnesses would condemn Jesus before the chief priest at His trial.

The Lord continued to be with Joseph and he rose to leadership in prison, just as he had in Potiphar's house. "[T]he keeper of the prison committed to Joseph's hand all the prisoners that were in the prison." This authority eventually brought him in contact with Pharaoh's butler and baker. The details of their offenses against Pharaoh are not given, but they were serious enough that Pharaoh had "put them in ward," meaning they were under a type of house arrest rather than incarcerated in the dungeons.

One night, the butler and the baker each had a dream. The butler dreamed of a "vine" with three branches. The vine budded, blossomed, and brought forth grapes. In the dream, the butler pressed the grapes, put the juice into Pharaoh's cup, and gave it to Pharaoh to drink. Joseph interpreted the dream as follows: the three branches represented three days, after which Pharaoh would restore the butler to his former position. Joseph then told the butler how he had been stolen from his own land and had done nothing to warrant his imprisonment, and he asked the butler to remember him so that he too might be released from prison.

The baker, upon hearing the favorable interpretation of the butler's dream, eagerly told Joseph *his* dream. In his dream he saw three baskets on his head. The top basket held various "bakemeats" for Pharaoh, but birds came and ate them up. Joseph interpreted the baker's dream, but it was not good news. "The three baskets are three days," he said. "Yet within three days shall Pharaoh lift up thy head from off thee, and shall hang thee on a tree; and the birds shall eat thy flesh from off thee"—all came to pass just as Joseph predicted. Furthermore, the feckless butler forgot to help Joseph and he had to remain in prison for two more years. No details are given of his activities during that time.

At this point in the story Pharaoh has his famous dreams: first, of the "seven well favoured kine" and the seven "ill favored" kine that consumed them; and second, of seven ears of good corn being devoured by seven ears of thin corn. Pharaoh was troubled by these dreams and called for his magicians and wise men to interpret them—but they could not. On cue, however, the butler propitiously remembered Joseph. He told Pharaoh how Joseph had interpreted his dream while he was in ward. Pharaoh sent to the prison for Joseph, and the scripture notes that Joseph hastily "shaved himself, and changed his raiment," before he went before Pharaoh. During their audience, Pharaoh revealed that he had been told that Joseph could interpret dreams, and Joseph answered that it was not him, but God, who would provide an interpretation and give Pharaoh peace.

Pharaoh recited his dreams to Joseph, and Joseph told him that God had told Pharaoh what He was about to do. Joseph's interpretation revealed that there would be seven years of plenty in Egypt followed by seven years of famine. Perhaps thinking of himself for the position, Joseph advised Pharaoh to find a counselor and administrator who could lay up stores during the good years in preparation for the years of famine. Not surprisingly, Pharaoh appointed Joseph to this position. "Thou shalt be over my house, and according unto thy word shall all my people be ruled: only in the throne will I be greater than thou," Pharaoh said. He gave Joseph his ring, arrayed him in proper "vestures of fine linen, and put a gold chain about his neck," and had him ride in the second chariot, so that people would "bow the knee" before him. Thus Joseph arose once more from obscurity to prominence in Egypt. Then Pharaoh changed Joseph's name to Zaphnath-paaneah (which no one remembers) and gave him Asenath, the daughter of the priest of On, as his wife. They eventually become the parents of two sons: Manasseh, the firstborn, and Ephraim.

As predicted, after seven productive years along came seven years of famine. Joseph arranged to have food stored throughout the seven years of plenty and during the famine he controlled its distribution to all who needed it. Through payments extracted for the food (the priests being excluded from payment), he eventually acquired both the wealth and the land of Egypt for Pharaoh, which put the Egyptians under bondage to their rulers—much like the bondage that would eventually befall the Israelites. The famine extended beyond Egypt and into Canaan and the story now turns to Joseph's brothers and his father, Jacob.

Because of the famine in Canaan, Jacob sent ten of his sons to Egypt to buy corn, but he kept the youngest son, Benjamin, at home. When the brothers gained audience before Joseph, Joseph recognized them, but they did not recognize him. And the dreams of his youth were fulfilled as the brothers bowed themselves down before him "with their faces to the earth" in obeisance. Joseph questioned them and "spake roughly unto them," accusing them of being spies. To refute his accusations, they told Joseph about their background and their families and in the telling, eventually informed Joseph that his father and younger brother, Benjamin, still lived. Joseph permitted them to buy corn upon the condition that Benjamin would be brought to him. He decreed that one of the brothers must retrieve Benjamin while the other nine waited in prison. Joseph then put them in "ward" for three days to think about it.

After the third day Joseph reduced the requirements: one brother would remain in Egypt as a hostage while the others would deliver the grain they had purchased to their families and then return with Benjamin. By this Joseph declared that he would know they were not spies, but "true men," and thereafter they could "traffick in the land." Simeon was to remain in Egypt, and Joseph had him bound. The sacks of the brothers were filled with grain but unbeknownst to them, Joseph had their payment money placed in the top of each of their sacks which (when found) produced great fear among them. Nonetheless, they returned to their father and told him all that had happened and what Joseph required of them.

At first Jacob refused to send Benjamin to Joseph, but Reuben and Judah stepped forward. Reuben offered to vouch for the safe return of Benjamin, stipulating that his two sons would be slain if Benjamin was not returned unharmed. Jacob again refused. Then Judah reiterated the fact that Benjamin was required to go, and he offered himself and his possessions as "surety" for Benjamin. Finally convinced, Jacob provided double payment to pay for the new corn and to reimburse Joseph for the money that had been found in the brothers' grain sacks. In addition, he prepared a present to be given to Joseph. With that, Benjamin was allowed to accompany his brothers back to Egypt.

When the brothers arrived in Egypt, Joseph's steward informed them that he was to take them to Joseph's house and there they would dine with Joseph. They became frightened and informed the servant that they had found their previous payment in their sacks and did not know how it got there. Further, they told him that they had brought double payment with them. The servant restored Simeon to them from prison, informed them that it was he who had restored their money, and that they should not be afraid because their God was with them. They prepared the present for Joseph and awaited his arrival. Joseph arrived at noon for the feast and when they were settled, the brothers gave him their present and again bowed low before him.

The feast began, but the participants were seated apart from each other, perhaps even in different areas. Joseph was seated alone, his eleven brothers were seated together but in a different area, and some unidentified Egyptian guests were seated separately in yet a third area. The scriptures only mention the reason for the seating arrangement of the Egyptians because they were prohibited from eating with Hebrews, for it was "an abomination unto [them]." Undoubtedly Joseph was seated alone because he was the ruler of all Egypt, while his brothers were but cautious guests. Joseph had his brothers seated according to their "birthright," or age, and Benjamin was served five times the normal portion—all to the astonishment of his brothers.

Soon after the feast the brothers leave for home with full sacks of grain for their father and families—and again their money is placed in the top of their sacks. However, this time Joseph puts his "divining" cup in the top of Benjamin's sack. The Greeks called the use of a divining cup "hydromancy," a way of foretelling events by observing the surface motion of wine in a special cup.[62] The practice was later forbidden and condemned under the Law of Moses. (Deuteronomy 18:10–11.) Joseph sends his guards to "find his cup," and they (after finding the cup in Benjamin's sack) force the brothers to return to Egypt. In the presence of Joseph, Judah steps forward and informs him of all that has transpired, including the fact that he is "surety" for Benjamin's safe return to their father. Finally, Joseph can withhold himself from his brothers no longer. He weeps in private and then reveals his true identity to them. He instructs them to return to their land and bring Jacob and their families back to Egypt so that he can provide for them, because "God hath made me lord of all Egypt."

Jacob, after hearing all that has transpired and learning that Joseph, his favorite son, is alive, rejoices exceedingly and sets out for Egypt. Along the way he stops at Beersheba and offers "sacrifices unto the God of his father Isaac." God responds by telling Jacob to go to Egypt, "for I will there make of thee a great nation," He promises, and "I will also surely bring thee up again." So all of Jacob's family, together with their possessions, leave for Egypt—sixty-six souls in all (including Joseph, his wife, and their two sons, Jacob's family now totals seventy souls). And because they were shepherds, they were given the land of Goshen where there was good pasture for their herds.

---

[62] The Torah: A Modern Commentary p. 278.

The record of the Israelites' sojourn in Egypt now jumps from episode to episode:

- Jacob is taken before Pharaoh and he blesses him.
- Jacob is cited as being one hundred and thirty years old.
- Another ten years pass without detail and Jacob is close to death. He calls Joseph to him and adopts Joseph's sons, Manasseh and Ephraim, into the house of Israel—as if they were his own sons. (He tells Joseph that only the sons born after Ephraim and Manasseh would be considered *Joseph's* sons.)
- Placing his right hand on Ephraim's head and his left on Manasseh's head, Jacob then blesses the boys. Joseph attempts to correct the hand placement because it would cause the younger boy to receive the birthright blessing, but Jacob states that he knows what he is doing. He tells Joseph that Ephraim will be greater than Manasseh, and Ephraim's seed shall become a "multitude of nations."
- Jacob then calls all of his twelve sons to him and gives each of them a patriarchal blessing.
- Although each of the sons received a blessing, the future of Israel as a nation is only revealed through two of them— the blessings of Judah and Joseph. Perhaps Judah because of his willingness to sacrifice himself for the protection of Benjamin and Joseph, because he was the firstborn of Rebekah, Jacob's favorite wife (whom he intended to be his first wife).
- The kings of Israel would arise through Judah, and eventually Christ would be born through his linage.
- Joseph was given the birthright, the blessings of the Covenant of Abraham, perhaps presaged by the earlier blessing of Ephraim when he was made the birthright son of Joseph and the adopted son of Jacob.
- After completing the blessings and indicating his desire to be buried with Abraham, Isaac, "Rebekah his wife," and Leah, Jacob passes away.

Joseph wept at his father's death and had him embalmed in the manner of the Egyptians. He asked Pharaoh to allow him and his family to carry Jacob to the land of Canaan for burial "in the cave of the field of Machpelah . . . before Memre."

After the burial Joseph and the family return to Egypt. However, the brothers feared that now their father was dead, Joseph would retaliate for their having sold him into slavery. But Joseph forgave them (another similitude of Jesus forgiving the Romans who crucified Him). This act of forgiveness is evidence of Joseph's greatness. It reveals the development of his character—from his recurring trials and suffering, through the depth of his personal humility, to the strong convictions of his deeply rooted faith in God.

Joseph lived to see Ephraim's children to the third generation, as well as those of Machir, the son of Manasseh. As his death approached, he told his brethren "God will surely visit you, and bring you out of this land unto the land which he sware to Abraham, to Isaac, and to Jacob." And he made them covenant that they would carry his bones with them when they went.

Joseph is one of the great figures of the Old Testament. No evil of any kind is attributed to him. He is constantly rising from precarious situations that could have led to his complete downfall to ever greater positions. He never took retribution on anyone. The scriptures identify those who harmed Joseph, but other than his brothers, you never hear of them again: the Midianites who bought and sold him, Potiphar and his duplicitous wife, and the feckless butler who forgot Joseph and left him in prison for two years. Although the story indicates that Joseph had some *fun* with his brothers as he maneuvered to see Benjamin and Jacob, he took no vengeance against them. He gracefully forgave them for all they had done to him, indicating that God had guided their actions in order to save their lives and the lives of many others. When he died, Joseph was one hundred and ten years old. As was then customary in Egypt, he was embalmed and "put in a coffin" to await the long years until the children of Israel could take him home.

Thus ends Genesis and the stories of the Prophet-Patriarchs—from the creation of the man Adam to the creation of the nation Israel.[63]

---

[63] See the Prophet-Patriarchs Time Line.

Section II
United Israel

This is the period of Israel that includes the life of Moses and runs through the reign of King Solomon. It begins with the book of Exodus, formally named: *THE SECOND BOOK OF MOSES, CALLED EXODUS.*

Although the *house* of Israel existed from the birth of Jacob's first son, Israel as a *nation*—both temporally and spiritually—did not come into being until the Exodus. The scriptures reveal that through this entire period of development, friction between individuals and tribes caused it to struggle within itself, from its enslavement up to the monarchies of David and Solomon. Although Israel survived as a nation for approximately 300 years, it finally collapsed as a united kingdom at the death of Solomon, in approximately 975 B.C.

Moses

circa 1300 B.C.[64]
Exodus, Leviticus, Numbers, Deuteronomy, Moses 1, 2

M oses was born sometime in the thirteenth century B.C. and died in the early part of the twelfth century B.C.[65] In addition to the first five books in the Bible and the book of Moses, there are many references concerning him throughout the scriptures. In Genesis, Moses recorded the historical rendering of God's dealings with the human race from the story of the creation through the patriarchs and concluded with the death of Joseph in Egypt. In Exodus we are introduced to Moses the man, but the stories in Exodus and in the balance of the Pentateuch are not primarily about Moses, they're about God and God's dealings with the people of Israel.

There are only ten verses in Exodus that relate the childhood of Moses, and only twelve that describe his adulthood prior to his call by God. He was from the tribe of Levi, the son of Amram and Jochebed, and he was born in Goshen on the Nile Delta under the harshest of edicts. Egyptians had been placed as taskmasters over the children of Israel because they had grown so numerous. Pha-

---

[64] Dating Moses has varied. This date is based on the acceptance of the 400-year term of enslavement of the children of Israel in Egypt and is in agreement with the Jewish calculation. The dates of the prophets until Samuel are based on this assumption. From Samuel forward, the Jewish calculation and others generally agree.

[65] Catholic Encyclopedia: Moses; The Torah: A Modern Commentary, p. 363 et seq.

raoh was concerned that they would soon outnumber the Egyptians, so an edict was given that all of the Israelites' male children were to be killed. But Godfearing Israelite midwives would not comply, forcing Pharaoh to set his own people to the task of casting every male Israelite child into the river to drown.

The story of how Moses was saved from this fate is well-known. His mother concealed him for three months. But when it was no longer possible to hide the child, she placed him in an "ark of bulrushes, and daubed it with slime and with pitch" and placed it in the "flags" near the river's bank. The daughter of Pharaoh found the baby and had mercy on him. Moses' sister, who had been secretly watching over her brother, suggested a nurse for him from among the Hebrew women. So it was that the mother of Moses was cleverly "pressed into service" to care for him until he was weaned. The daughter of Pharaoh named the child Moses, meaning *drawn,* because she had drawn him out of the water. Thereafter, he was raised in the palace of Pharaoh and educated in "all the wisdom of the Egyptians."

We hear nothing more of Moses until he reaches manhood when, as he was observing the burdens of "his brethren," he killed an Egyptian for beating a Hebrew slave. The next day as he tried to resolve a conflict between two Hebrews, his efforts were rebuffed when one of the contenders responded: "Who made thee a prince and a judge over us?" Do you intend to "kill me, as thou killedst the Egyptian?" Moses thought no one had seen him when he killed the Egyptian and buried him. But now he knew there had been a witness to his deed. By some unknown means, news of Moses' crime had made its way to the ears of Pharaoh and he sought to kill Moses. However, by fleeing into the land of Midian, Moses escaped from Pharaoh's judgment.

During his stay in Midian, Moses met the seven daughters of Reuel (Jethro) at a well and assisted them in fending off some marauders who were after their flocks. He eventually married one of the daughters, a woman named Zipporah, and they named their firstborn son Gershom.

One day as Moses tended his father-in-law's flocks on Mount Horeb, "the angel of the Lord appeared unto him in a flame of fire out of the midst of a bush" which was not consumed. The Lord called the eighty-year-old Moses to be his prophet and commanded him to go to Pharaoh and demand freedom for the children of Israel. Moses questioned the Lord, asking how the Israelites would recognize that God had sent him. The Lord told him to tell them that "I AM" had sent him, a name they would recognize.

The Lord prepared Moses for this mission by providing him with some of the miraculous signs that he would eventually present to Pharaoh. He turned Moses' rod into a serpent—then back into a rod. He made the hand of Moses leprous—then well again. And if Pharaoh would not believe these signs, Moses was to take water from the Nile River and pour it on the ground where it would turn into blood. Moses hesitated, declaring that he was "not eloquent . . . but I am slow of speech . . . and of a slow tongue." The Lord promised Moses that He would be with him and teach him what to say.

When Enoch was called by the Lord, he had complained about being "slow of speech." But the Lord blessed Enoch with the same blessing that He now promised Moses: "Open thy mouth, and it shall be filled, and I will give thee utterance." But while Enoch accepted the Lord's promised blessing on faith, Moses would not.

God became angry when Moses rejected His offer and withdrew His promised blessing. Instead, He called Moses' brother Aaron to be mouth for him declaring, "he (Aaron) shall be thy spokesman unto the people: and he shall be . . . to thee instead of a mouth, and thou shall be to him instead of God." From that point on, the history of Moses reflects the birth of the nation of Israel as the Lord inflicts plague after plague upon Egypt. He ultimately sends the angel of death upon all the firstborn of Egypt to force Pharaoh to release Israel's children. But the job would not be simple as we shall see.

◆ ◆ ◆

Perhaps when Moses embarked on his mission he thought his task would be easy. He went before Pharaoh and demanded that Pharaoh let the people go. Pharaoh haughtily refused saying: "Who is the Lord, that I should obey his voice?" Thereafter he increased the onerous tasks upon the Hebrew slaves by requiring them to provide their own straw for the bricks they made, even though their quota remained the same. Because of this, the officers of the Israelites who had been appointed by the Egyptian taskmasters complained to Moses and Aaron.

Moses went before the Lord wondering why He had allowed the burdens of His children to increase and why Pharaoh had not let the children go. He asked, "why is it that thou has sent me?" The Lord responded by declaring that His name was JEHOVAH and that He would make Israel His people and He would be their God. He commanded Moses to return to Pharaoh, stating that from then on Moses would be "a god to Pharaoh," and his brother Aaron would be Moses' "prophet."

To witness God's power, Aaron cast down his rod before Pharaoh and it became a serpent. But Pharaoh's magicians duplicated the feat with their enchantments. Nonetheless, Aaron's serpent devoured the serpents of the magicians. This did not particularly impress Pharaoh, and he hardened his heart even more.

The plagues began when Moses turned the waters to blood. The magicians again performed their enchantments and duplicated the sign. When the Lord plagued Egypt with frogs, the magicians replicated God's effort. But when all of the dust of Egypt was turned into lice, the magicians could not duplicate the miracle and confessing their lack of ability, they solemnly proclaimed, "This is the finger of God."

Up to this point, the plagues had fallen on Egyptian and Israelite alike. But with the plague of flies, the Lord "sever[ed] . . . the land of Goshen," and the plagues fell only upon the Egyptians. Through boils with blains that fell upon man and beast; hail that turned to fire and ran along the ground; locusts that left "not any green thing in the trees, or in the herbs of the field";

and thick darkness that covered the land for three days; Pharaoh vacillated between promising to set Israel free as his people suffered, and hardening his heart when a plague abated. Finally, Pharaoh had had enough of Moses: "Get thee from me," he commanded. "See my face no more; for in that day thou seest my face thou shalt die." After that edict, Moses left Pharaoh alone. But there was still one more plague that would beset the Egyptians.

The Lord then instructed the elders of Israel as follows: "This month shall be unto you the beginning of months . . . the first month of the year to you." He told them to select an unblemished lamb on the tenth day of the month and keep it until the fourteenth day. On that day, they were to slaughter the lamb and paint some of its blood on the two side posts and the upper door post of the house wherein the lamb would be eaten—along with unleavened bread and bitter herbs. He said if any of the meat was left over when morning came, they were to burn it with fire. Moreover, during the meal they were to be fully dressed, their feet shod, and their staves in their hands ready for travel. And they were to eat hastily, for it was the Lord's "Passover."

And then the plague came. At midnight on the day appointed, the spirit of the Lord went throughout the land of Egypt and slew the firstborn child of every family, from the family of the great Pharaoh to that of the captive in his dank dungeons. The firstborn of beasts were also destroyed. But none of the Israelites' families were harmed because the angel of death "passed by" the homes whose lintels had been painted with lamb's blood. However, "there was a great cry in Egypt; for there was not a house where there was not one dead." The Lord instructed Israel to remember this day as a "memorial," and keep it as a feast for "an ordinance for ever."

Overwhelmed by the sweeping impact of this last, devastating plague, Pharaoh finally capitulated and let the Israelites go. In preparation, the Lord commanded the children of Israel to borrow everything they could from the Egyptians for He would "spoil"

Egypt. And then, after four hundred and thirty years, six hundred thousand Israelites (not counting women and children) left Egypt. "A mixed multitude went up also with them; and flocks, and herds, even very much cattle. And they baked unleavened cakes of the dough which they brought forth out of Egypt . . . because they were thrust out of Egypt, and could not tarry, neither had they prepared for themselves any victual."

In spite of the costly and demoralizing death of Egypt's first-born, Pharaoh and his servants soon wondered why they had let Israel go from "serving them." No matter what the cost, they wanted slaves. So Pharaoh took six hundred chariots with their captains and pursued the children of Israel. They overtook the Israelites as they camped by the sea. The formidable array of chariots caused the children of Israel to cry unto the Lord—but to Moses they said, "Because there were no graves in Egypt, hast thou taken us away to die in the wilderness? . . . Is not this the word that we did tell thee in Egypt, saying, Let us alone, that we may serve the Egyptians?" They had been content as slaves, but Moses would have none of that. "Stand still," he commanded, "and see the salvation of the Lord." Although they could see the threatening power of the Egyptians, Moses promised them that they would "see them again no more for ever."

The Lord seemed agitated when He said to Moses, "Wherefore criest thou unto me? [S]peak unto the children of Israel, that they go forward." He commanded Moses to stretch his hand over the sea and "divide it," so that the Israelites could go forward on "dry ground." "And the angel of God" and the "pillar of the cloud" which had been going before the camp, "removed and went behind them," between the camp of the Egyptians and the camp of Israel. Moses stretched forth his hand and the waters parted "by a strong east wind." The children of Israel marched into the cleft, "and the waters were a wall unto them on their right hand, and on their left," and the seabed was dry ground.

The Egyptians pursued Israel into the sea, but the Lord "troubled" them, and removed the wheels of their chariots. When all of the Israelites were on the other side of the sea, the Lord once again commanded Moses to stretch forth his hand and the sea closed in above the Egyptians and their horses and their chariots—completely destroying them. The children of Israel stopped complaining when they "saw that great work which the Lord did upon the Egyptians: and the people feared the LORD, and believed the LORD, and his servant Moses." Little wonder!

Where Moses led the people into the wilderness, food was scarce. Again the people complained. "We were better off in Egypt!" they grumbled. There we had "bread to the full." Now you will "kill this whole assembly with hunger." But the Lord told Moses that he would "rain bread from heaven" for them. Each day they could gather only enough to satisfy their needs for that day, but no more. On the sixth day they could gather twice as much, for none could be gathered on the Sabbath. That evening the Lord sent quail to the camp so the Israelites would have meat to eat one more day. In the morning there "lay a small round thing" on the ground that was white like coriander seed and tasted like wafers made with honey. They called it "manna." They had to hurry and collect it in the morning, for as the "sun waxed hot, it melted." Nevertheless, some delayed in their collection and the manna "bred worms, and stank."

But in time, the people grew weary of just eating manna. They wanted meat! "Who shall give us flesh to eat?" they asked, "for it was well with us in Egypt." A terse reply came from the Lord: "Ye shall not eat [meat] one day, nor two days, nor five days, neither ten days, nor twenty days; But even a whole month, until it come out at your nostrils, and it be loathsome unto you."[66] And the Lord brought quail to the camp until they were piled up "two

---

[66] Numbers 11:20.

cubits high upon the face of the earth." When the manna returned, the people rejoiced and happily "did eat manna forty years."

Eventually Moses led the camp to Mount Sinai where God waited because Moses wanted them to enter the Lord's presence. He told them to sanctify themselves and wash their clothes; but the people became frightened when they saw the "thunders and lightnings, and a thick cloud upon the mount." The sound of a trumpet was heard and it grew louder and louder. When Moses spoke, God "answered him by a voice." The people were terrified and told Moses that he could speak with God, but "let not God speak with us, lest we die."

Moses went up on the mount and received diverse laws and ordinances from God. Then God commanded Moses (along with "Aaron, Nadab, and Abihu, and seventy of the elders of Israel") to come upon the mountain together. There they "saw the God of Israel." Then the Lord commanded Moses to come up and receive the tablets of stone upon which were inscribed all of the commandments that God had given him. Moses stayed on the mountain, fasting, for forty days and forty nights before he started back with the tablets of stone. While he was away from the people, they again strayed. They induced Aaron to forge a golden calf for them—and they "offered burnt offerings, and brought peace offerings; and [they] sat down to eat and to drink, and rose up to play." And God commanded Moses to return to the camp because the people had "corrupted themselves."

God was angry with the children of Israel. He told Moses that He would destroy all of Israel because of its wickedness, after which He would make of Moses a great nation. But Moses pled for the children of Israel until the Lord changed his mind. When he returned to the camp and saw the calf and the dancing, Moses' anger "waxed hot." He broke the tablets before the people, ground the golden calf into powder, "strawed it upon the water," and made the people drink of it. Later, the Lord commanded Moses to return to the mount and make new tablets so that he could again obtain the Lord's commandments that were on the first tablets.

"And the Lord spake unto Moses face to face, as a man speaketh unto his friend."

Moses took the people to the borders of the Promised Land and sent spies into the land to reconnoiter it. When the spies returned from their journey, they were all afraid—except Joshua and Caleb, who returned carrying a huge grape cluster so heavy they had to suspend it on a pole between them. They begged the people to follow them into the Promised Land, but they would not budge. Because they refused to move, the Lord exiled them to the wilderness for forty years until all the older generation of Israelites, except Joshua and Caleb, had aged and died.

The rest of Moses' story involves travel and travail as he leads the Israelites through the wilderness. Miracles occurred almost daily. Not only did manna continue to appear each morning, but the company's clothes and shoes did not wear out nor get old.[67] Moses continually received instructions from God on how to guide the people. Under the Lord's direction he built the Tabernacle which contained the Ark of the Covenant in which was housed the tablets of the ten commandments and the pot of manna which the Lord had commanded them to preserve. He inaugurated the Levitical Priesthood and the Priesthood of Aaron; he initiated the Law of Moses, established sacrifice, and brought back circumcision as the sign of the covenant between Israel and God; he won a war by holding up his hands (albeit with some help); and he brought water from the rock "in Horeb," but he became angry with the people and didn't credit God sufficiently, so was punished by not being allowed to enter the Promised Land. But most of all, he made Israel a covenant people!

Moses' prophecies are almost as numerous as his miracles. He prophesied the coming of Jesus and the persecution, scattering and gathering of Israel. He taught the Israelites that they would

---

[67] Deuteronomy 29:5.

be blessed for obedience to God's commandments, and cursed if they disobeyed them. He received vision after vision, including one of the "world and the ends thereof, and all the children of men which are, and which were created." He even saw Satan and was tempted by him.

Moses was so conversant with God that he asked *HIM* questions. "Tell me, I pray thee," he queried after seeing the great visions of all the heavens and the earth, "why these things are so, and by what thou madest them?" In answer, God revealed the glorious revelation of the creation of the earth and the creation of man, the first flesh thereon. "There was not a soul which [Moses] beheld not."

In the New Testament, Moses appeared with Elijah on the Mount of Transfiguration to commune with the Savior.[68] During the restoration, he appeared in the Kirtland Temple to Joseph Smith and Oliver Cowdery "and committed unto [them] the keys of the gathering of Israel from the four parts of the earth, and the leading of the ten tribes from the land of the north."[69] He instituted the two great commandments upon which Jesus said all the law and the prophets would hang:[70] first, ". . . *thou shalt love the Lord thy God* with all thine heart, and with all thy soul, and with all thy might,"[71] and second, "Thou shalt not avenge, nor bear any grudge against the children of thy people, but *thou shalt love thy neighbour as thyself*" (emphasis added).[72] Because he lived in constant touch with God, it was said that Moses "was very meek, above all the men which were upon the face of the earth."[73]

It is almost impossible to describe all that Moses was. At the ripe old age of one hundred and twenty, he pronounced a prophetic blessing upon each of the twelve tribes of Israel, just as Jacob had done before him. Then he hiked from the plains of Moab up to the mountain of Nebo, "to the top of Pisgah." The scripture states that from that vantage point, the Lord showed him

68 Matthew 17:1–8.
69 Doctrine & Covenants 110:11.
70 Matthew 22:40.
71 Deuteronomy 6:5.
72 Leviticus 19:18.
73 Numbers 12:3.

the fruitful land He had promised Abraham, Isaac, and Jacob. *Moses could see this choice land, but could not enter it.* In accordance with the word of the Lord, he was destined to die in the land of Moab. The Lord buried him in a valley in the land of Moab over against Bethpeor: but no one knows where his sepulcher is to this day. Thereafter it was said of him, "there arose not a prophet since in Israel like unto Moses, whom the Lord knew face to face."

Miriam the Prophetess

circa 1300 B.C.
Exodus 2:4–8; 15:20, 21; Numbers 12:1–15; 26:59

Miriam, the older sister of Moses and Aaron, was the only daughter of Amram and Jochebed. Her name has no established meaning, but has been interpreted over the years as *wished for child, bitter, rebellious, rebellion, beloved, defiant,* or *God's gift* by various scholars.[74] Perhaps all these names reflect her personality and character or come as a result of the known events of her life rather than the technical meaning of her name.

Although the scriptures don't mention her name in the story of Pharaoh's daughter, it is assumed that it was Miriam who spoke to the daughter when she found three-month-old Moses floating in an ark made of bullrushes near the banks of the Nile River. Hoping to save his life, Moses' mother had placed him in the river lest he be killed under Pharaoh's edict to destroy all the male children of the Israelites. The scripture notes that Miriam "stood afar off, to wit[ness] what would be done to him." When the child cried, Pharaoh's daughter found him and had compassion on him even though she knew he was a Hebrew. Miriam spoke with her and suggested that a nurse of the Hebrew women be found to care for the child and Pharaoh's daughter agreed. Miriam then retrieved

[74] Smith's Bible Dictionary: Miriam, Columbia Encyclopedia: Sermon by Dr. James L. Wilson.

Moses' mother, and she raised him until he was weaned. It would therefore seem logical to assume that the placing of Moses in the ark, his discovery by Pharaoh's daughter, and the selection of Moses' mother as a wet nurse were not serendipitous events, but rather a clever plan on the part of Moses' parents.

We don't know how old Miriam was during the story of Moses' discovery, but she was old enough to participate in the plot to save Moses. Nothing else is said of her until the story of the Exodus begins some eighty years later.

After the crossing of the sea on dry land, the scriptures note that Moses sang a song praising the Lord for the successful crossing of the sea and the destruction of Pharaoh's armies. After Moses finished his song, "Miriam the prophetess, the sister of Aaron, took a timbrel in her hand; and all the women went out after her with timbrels and with dances." She is the first woman (and only one of three that are identified by name)[75] to be referred to as a "prophetess" in the scriptures. She commands the women saying, "Sing ye to the Lord, for he hath triumphed gloriously; the horse and his rider hath he thrown into the sea," thus expressing her prophetic calling in poetry, music, and processions.

Nothing more is said of Miriam until the episode when she and Aaron question the leadership of Moses. They were complaining because Moses had taken an Ethiopian woman as a wife, and they criticized his judgment. They said they were in a better position to receive direction from the Lord in the matter than Moses was, and they questioned his leadership as the prophet of Israel. "Hath the Lord indeed spoken only by Moses?" they asked. "Hath he not spoken also to us?" It's clear from their confrontational attitude that they felt Moses was in the wrong for having taken an Ethiopian in marriage.

The Lord "spake suddenly unto Moses, and unto Aaron, and unto Miriam," and called them to the tabernacle. He came down

[75] Although Noadiah is identified as a prophetess, because of her actions in the conspiracy against Nehemiah, she is identified as a false prophetess herein.

in a "pillar of the cloud, and stood in the door of the tabernacle" as He called Miriam and Aaron forth. Then the Lord told them that it was He who would call the prophet. And it was He who would make Himself known in "vision," and in dreams, and would "speak mouth to mouth" with His prophet. And the prophet would behold the "similitude of the Lord." The Lord became angry with Miriam and Aaron, and although they had both questioned Moses, only Miriam received the corporal punishment—she became "leprous, white as snow"—perhaps a firm indication that she was the instigator of the rebellion against Moses since even though Aaron participated, he went unpunished.

Aaron became submissive to Moses, called him "my lord," and pled forgiveness for his participation in the "sin" against his younger brother. He asked Moses to call upon the Lord to heal Miriam. (Perhaps this mental anguish, confession, and subjection to Moses were a greater punishment for his participation in the rebellion than Miriam's corporal punishment). Moses had compassion for them both and Miriam was healed, but she "was shut out from the camp seven days." The camp of Israel "journeyed not" until she had completed her personal exile.

This event is the last we know of Miriam's life. There are two other times when she is mentioned in the Bible: first is a warning by Moses that the children of Israel should remember what the Lord did to Miriam because of her questioning and disobedience,[76] and the second is a reminder of her contribution when the Lord brought Israel out of Egypt's bondage as recounted by Micah.[77]

Because there are so few actual facts known about Miriam, many myths and stories have grown up over the centuries. According to tradition, she prophesied to her parents that one would be born to them who would redeem Israel from bondage. Another myth is that she was the ancestress of Bezalel of the tribe of Judah who designed the tabernacle (even though Miriam was of

[76] Deuteronomy 24:9.   [77] Micah 6:4.

the tribe of Levi). Another tradition says a well of fresh water followed the camp until her death.[78]

Miriam, as with Aaron and Moses, did not cross over Jordan and enter the Promised Land. She died in Kadesh and was buried there.[79]

---

[78] Judaism 101 by Tracey R. Rich.

[79] Numbers 20:1.

Joshua/Oshea

1250 B.C.

Exodus 17:9–14; 24:13; 32:17; 33:11; Numbers 13:8, 16–30;
14:30; 27:18–23; Joshua

The name Joshua means *savior* or *whose help is Jehovah.* Joshua is also known by the name Oshea which means *salvation.* He was the immediate successor of Moses. Moses confirmed this when he laid his hands upon Joshua "before Eleazar the priest, and before all the congregation"; and gave him the charge and authority to lead all Israel.[80]

The first thing the Lord did after the death of Moses and the thirty days of mourning that followed was to speak to Joshua and command him to cross over Jordan and possess the promised land. God assured Joshua that "as I was with Moses, so I will be with thee: I will not fail thee, nor forsake thee." The Lord further exhorted him to "Be strong and of a good courage." He reminded Joshua to do all that the Law of Moses commanded, stating that if he would but comply, the "book of the law shall not depart out of thy mouth; but thou shalt meditate therein day and night, that thou mayest observe to do according to all that is written therein."

As Joshua approached Jordan (with the Ark of the Covenant at the head of the caravan), the Lord spoke with him and promised that he would magnify him in the sight of the whole company so that the Israelites would know, "as I was with Moses, so I will be with thee."

[80] Numbers 27:18–23; Deuteronomy 34:9.

Joshua "said unto the children of Israel, Come hither, and hear the words of the Lord your God." He then told them that when the priests entered Jordan, the waters of Jordan would "stand upon an heap"—in other words, stop flowing—so that the children of Israel could cross over on dry ground, just as their fathers had crossed the Red Sea some forty years earlier. This miracle was given as a testimony so that the Israelites would know that: "the living God [was] among [them]." And as the waters parted, they knew that He was.

Joshua was the military leader of Israel both before and after Moses' death. When Moses held up his hands to determine whether the armies of Israel would have defeat or victory in their battle with the Amalekites, it was Joshua who led the attack.

Joshua renewed the law of circumcision which had been ignored during the exodus and was present when the gift of manna came to an end. As he prepared for the battle of Jericho, a man stood before him with his sword drawn in his hand. It was the "captain of the host of the Lord" and Joshua, just as Moses, was commanded to take off his shoes because the Lord said, the "place whereon thou standest is holy." Then the Lord instructed him on how to capture Jericho, a walled city in the valley of the Jordan River, 800 feet below the Mediterranean Sea. The Lord told Joshua to "compass" the city and circle it once a day for six days with the men of war and the priests bearing the Ark of the Covenant, and carrying their trumpets and ram's horns. Each day they blew on the trumpets and ram's horns, but Joshua told the rest of the army to "not shout, nor make any noise with your voice." On the seventh day the procedure changed. The army rose early and marched and marched around Jericho six times, and then seven priests bearing "seven trumpets of rams' horns" went before the Ark of the Covenant and led the army around the city one more time. When the army heard a long blast from the Priest's trumpets, they all shouted "a great shout; and the wall of the city fell down 'flat.'" Joshua, of course, won the day in this well-known story.

Joshua saw the Lord intervene on behalf of the Israelites over and over again. On one occasion He sent "hailstones" to destroy the Gibeonites, and another time He stopped the sun and moon in the valley of Ajalon until the Amorites were destroyed and Israel "avenged." King after king fell to Joshua as the local tribes were conquered. Finally, he was commanded to divide the land among the tribes of Israel, giving a portion to each of ten tribes and two portions to the tribe of Joseph via Jacob's adopted sons, Ephraim and Manasseh. But the tribe of Levi was given no portion of the land. Instead, the Levites received numerous cities and the tithes of the people to house and sustain them. Joshua gave Caleb, who helped him spy out the land of Canaan prior to the Lord sending the Israelites back into the wilderness for forty years, the ancient city of Hebron as an inheritance. (Hebron, in contrast to Jericho, was 3,040 feet above the Mediterranean Sea.) Caleb declared that at eighty-five, he was as "strong" as the day Moses sent him into Canaan with Joshua. "As my strength was then," he claimed, "even so is my strength now, for war, both to go out, and to come in." He had been fighting for Israel for forty-five years.

Because they were herdsmen and the land was covered with grass, two and a half tribes took their portion of land on the "other side" of Jordan. They promised Joshua that they would fight for Israel until the other tribes had their land if he would grant them their wish. The inheritance was granted. After their commitment was fulfilled, the men of Reuben, Gad, and half of Manasseh were released to return to their families with Joshua's blessing.

After many difficult battles, the Lord finally blessed Israel with peace. "A long time" passed after which Joshua called the people together, told them that he was getting old and "stricken in age," and gave them his last exhortation. He reminded them of all that God had done for them and gave them this challenge: "[I]f it seem evil unto you to serve the Lord, choose you this day whom ye will serve; whether the gods which your fathers served that were on the other side of the flood, or the gods of the Amorites, in whose land ye dwell: but as for me and my house, we will serve the Lord."

Israel's covenant with God was renewed when the people responded: "The Lord our God we will serve, and his voice will we obey."

"And it came to pass after these things, that Joshua the son of Nun, the servant of the Lord, died, being an hundred and ten years old." And the people buried him "in the border of his inheritance . . . in mount Ephraim, on the north side of the hill of Gaash."

Deborah the Prophetess

1130 B.C.
Judges 4–5

The name Deborah means *a bee.*[81] Deborah is only mentioned in two chapters of the Book of Judges. She is called a prophetess in those chapters and the verses indicate that the people came to her for judgment. She was the only woman judge in the history of Israel.

Her fame came at a time when Israel had been "evil in the sight of the Lord." As a result, the Lord had given them over to Jabin, king of Canaan. The scriptures carefully note that Sisera was captain of the Canaanite army and that the army had "nine hundred chariots of iron" and had oppressed Israel for twenty years.

Only one event in Deborah's life is elaborated upon and no information is given as to how she received her information. She calls Barak (also the only time he is mentioned) and tells him God has commanded that he lead ten thousand men from Naphtali and ten thousand men from Zebulun to confront the armies of Sisera, and that the Lord will deliver them into his hand.

Barak was hesitant, but agreed to comply with Deborah's prophecy on the condition that she accompany him to battle. She readily agreed, but stated that by doing so, Barak would not receive the

---

[81] Smith's Bible Dictionary: Deborah.

glory of the victory, but that the Lord would "sell Sisera into the hand of a woman." Barak gathers together the thousands from Naphtali and Zebulun and Deborah commands him to engage Sisera's forces, "for this is the day in which the Lord hath delivered Sisera into thine hand."

The Lord "discomfited Sisera, and all his chariots" and his army, until "there was not a man left," and Sisera fled to the tent of a woman named Jael and requested she give him sanctuary. She gave him milk to drink and covered him as he rested. He asked her to lie to anyone who inquired about him and say he was not in her tent. Then he promptly fell asleep.

Jael took a tent peg and while Sisera slept, she killed him by hammering the tent peg through his temples and into the ground. When Barak arrived, she went out to meet him and showed him all that she had done.

Barak and the army pursued Jabin, king of Canaan, until he was destroyed. Deborah and Barak composed and sang a victory song (just as Miriam had done) in celebration of the victory God had granted them. Nothing else is known about Deborah. We are not told of her birth nor of her death. The scriptures merely close by noting that after this battle, "the land had rest forty years."

Samuel

1050 B.C.
1 Samuel 1–25:1; 28:7–20

The name Samuel means: *heard of God, because I have asked him of the Lord.* He was born to a woman named Hannah under circumstances similar to those of Joseph of Egypt. Hannah was one of the two wives of Elkanah. The other wife's name was Peninnah. Peninnah had several children but like Rachel, Hannah was barren. The scripture notes carefully that Elkanah "loved" Hannah, just as Jacob loved Rachel. Each year Elkanah and the family would go up to worship and sacrifice in Shiloh at the tabernacle of the Lord. ("Temple" is used in this verse rather than tabernacle. However, the temple of Solomon had not yet been built; therefore, it was the *tabernacle* at which they worshiped.) Life was miserable for the childless wife in those days, and Hannah had a difficult time with an unnamed adversary— undoubtedly Peninnah—who "provoked her sore," so that Hannah "fret." It was on one of these trips to worship at the tabernacle that Hannah "wept sore" and was "in bitterness of soul," so she went to pray before the Lord. Eli, the high priest in Israel at the time, was sitting by a post of the tabernacle on a chair. From that vantage point he could observe Hannah in prayer. Hannah moved her lips but spake only in her heart. Her heart gave voice to her vow: if the Lord would grant her a male child, she would "give him unto the Lord all the days of his life," and no "rasor" would "come upon his head." In her vow she not only dedicated her son-to-be to the Lord, but she also swore that he would be a Nazarite from birth.

Eli "marked her mouth" and because her lips were moving without sound, he believed that she was drunk—and so accused her. Hannah denied the accusation saying that she had "poured out [her] soul before the Lord." Eli responded with kindness and although he did not know the request she had made, blessed her by saying, "the God of Israel grant thee thy petition that thou hast ask of him." The Lord harkened to Eli and remembered Hannah, as he had remembered Rachel. Shortly thereafter, Hannah bore a son and named him Samuel.

After the birth of Samuel, Hannah did not go up to Shiloh on the yearly anniversaries. She told Elkanah she would not go up until Samuel was weaned, and then she would leave him there as she had promised. Elkanah agreed, and once weaned, Samuel, who was perhaps only two years old, was carried by Hannah to the tabernacle of the Lord at Shiloh. In thanks to God, a bullock was slain and Hannah took the child to Eli and reminded him of her vow. Thereafter she "lent him to the Lord." An alternate translation for the word "lent" is rendered, "returned him, whom I have obtained by petition."[82]

Although not referred to as a prophetess, Hannah sang a song of thanksgiving (as Miriam and Deborah had done before her) for the *loan* (meaning the child) that God had loaned to her. Elkanah and Hannah returned to their home in Ramah. Samuel remained in Shiloh and ministered to the Lord with Eli the high priest. Yearly thereafter, Hannah would bring a new coat which she had made for Samuel. And the Lord blessed Hannah through Eli and she had three additional sons and two daughters.

Eli's sons, Hophni and Phinehas, were very wicked men. They extorted "donations" from those who came to sacrifice and they

---

[82] 1 Samuel 1:28: Alternate translation.

committed sins with the women who came to the door of the tabernacle. Eli chastised them, but he allowed them to continue judging and officiating in the office of priest—even though they did not repent of their sins. Through all of this, the only mention of Samuel is that "he grew . . . and was in favour both with the Lord, and also with men" (a comment similar to those concerning the early lives of both John the Baptist and Jesus).

After years of failure to correct his sons' sins, God sent an unnamed prophet to Eli to tell him of God's anger for allowing Hophni and Phinehas to continue in their sinful ways. He prophesied that both sons, Hophni and Phinehas, would die in one day and that Eli would have no progeny to succeed him. The man of God continued, prophesying that the Lord would raise up a "faithful priest" who would do all He asked of him—obviously referring to Samuel.

The testament does not tell us whether it was at this time or several years later that God called Samuel to be his prophet. The scriptures specifically note that *before* Samuel's call, the "word of the Lord was precious" and there was "no open vision."

At that time, one of the responsibilities of the high priest was to keep the "lamp of God" lit in the room where the Ark of the Covenant was located in the tabernacle (again referred to as the temple). Because Eli was old and blind, he had Samuel sleep in that room so that the lamp would not go out. It was on one of those nights that God spoke to the young boy, who was perhaps only twelve years of age at that time. When the Lord called to him, Samuel thought it was Eli calling and he ran to him crying, "Here am I." Eli awoke and said it was not he who had called. He told Samuel to return to bed. The Lord called a second time with the same result, and yet a third time. Although Samuel did not know it was the Lord's voice he was hearing, Eli understood what was occurring. He told Samuel to return to bed, and when the Lord called the fourth time, Samuel answered as he had been instructed.

The Lord's instructions to Samuel were not good news for Eli. The Lord condemned the sons of Eli for their sins and Eli for not correcting them. When morning came, Eli called Samuel and asked him what the Lord had said. Samuel was reluctant to tell him, but Eli persisted until Samuel told him all that the Lord had revealed. Eli confirmed it was the Lord who was speaking, and perhaps remembering the unnamed prophet's counsel and prophecy, and recognizing that he had not done what the Lord wanted, said: "It is the Lord: let him do what seemeth him good."

Another scripture (similar to that depicting the growing years of Jesus) says, "And Samuel grew, and the Lord was with him . . . And all Israel from Dan even to Beersheba knew that Samuel was established to be a prophet of the Lord." And the Lord even appeared and revealed Himself to Samuel in Shiloh.

Finally, the time came to "establish" Samuel as the judge and prophet in Israel. The Philistines had come to make war with Israel and they won the first battle. Thinking they would win if the Ark of the Covenant was in their midst, the armies of Israel sent for it. Hophni and Phinehas brought the Ark to the armies and the roaring shout signaling its arrival was so great that the earth "rang." When the Philistines heard the noise and were told that the Ark was in Israel's camp they became afraid. But their leaders encouraged them to be men and fight rather than become slaves of the Hebrews. The battle raged—and Israel was slaughtered. Thirty thousand Israelite footmen died in the conflict and the Ark was captured by the Philistines. The prophecy that the two sons of Eli would die was fulfilled as they fell in battle. When news of these catastrophic events was brought to Eli, he fell backward in his chair, broke his neck, and died. Eli had judged Israel for forty years.

✦ ✦ ✦

The story of the captured Ark is a story in and of itself. The Philistines put it in the "house" of Dagon, their god. In the morning they found that the statute of Dagon had fallen on its face before the Ark. They set Dagon aright, but by the next morning Dagon had fallen again. This time the palms of Dagon's hands and his head had been cut off and only his stump remained. Wherever the Ark went after that—through city after city— the people were beset with illness and death. Finally, the Philistines put the Ark on a cart drawn by two "milch kine," along with an offering of golden "emerods and mice," and sent it off toward Israel with the belief that if the milch kine took it toward Bethshemesh, it was the hand of the Lord that had caused all the Philistine's problems. If it went in a different direction, mere chance would have been the cause of their woes. Of course, the cart went to Bethshemesh. The people of Bethshemesh looked into the Ark, a forbidden act, and the Lord smote that city—fifty thousand and seventy men died. They immediately sent a message that the Philistines had returned the Ark . . . and would someone please come down and take it away.

Because they persisted in the worship of strange gods, including Ashtaroth, the goddess of fertility, all Israel had been in sin for decades. Samuel called them to Mizpeh where he rebuked them severely and called them to repentance. He promised that if they would repent, return to the Lord, put away their strange gods, prepare their hearts, and serve only the Lord, that the Lord would deliver them from the Philistines. They did as he asked! And when the Philistines came against Israel the Lord "thundered with a great thunder," and the Philistines were "smitten before Israel."

Samuel had two sons whom he placed on the judgment seat to judge Israel before he died, and just like Eli's sons, they were wicked and the people would not accept them. Further, the people came to Samuel and requested that he choose a king for them so that they could "be like all the nations." This request discomfited Samuel and he asked the Lord what he should do, but the Lord told him to do as the people had requested stating, "they have not rejected thee, but they have rejected me." They no longer wanted God to reign over them.

Under the direction of the Lord, Samuel selected a man named Saul to be the Israelites' king. The scriptures describe him as "a choice young man, and a goodly: there . . . not [being] among the children of Israel a goodlier person than he." Saul was from the tribe of Benjamin and "from his shoulders and upward," he was taller than anyone else in Israel.

Even after Saul was appointed and accepted by the people as their king, Samuel was not satisfied with the way things were going. He called Israel together and lectured the people. He chastised them because they had wanted and accepted a king, thereby rejecting him and the Lord. Finally, he told them they had made a gross mistake. To prove that, he called upon the Lord to confirm his words. The Lord sent "thunder and rain" upon them, and the scripture notes that the people "greatly feared the Lord and Samuel."

In the beginning Saul was a good king. But soon he became corrupted. One of his first mistakes was to offer the burnt offering to the Lord before a battle with the Philistines, rather than wait for Samuel to do it. Samuel arrived shortly thereafter and questioned why Saul had performed the sacrifice. As an excuse, Saul said he had forced himself to offer it because the people were running away. Samuel chastised Saul for acting "foolishly," and told him that because he had not kept the Lord's commandments, his reign over Israel would cease. Nevertheless, Saul continued his disobedience. When he was commanded by God (through Samuel) to destroy every living thing—both man and beast— of the Amalikites, he defiantly saved Agag, the Amalikite king, and kept the Amalikite sheep and cattle for sacrifice. Again Samuel was distraught and told Saul that although the Lord delighted in sacrifice, He was more delighted in being obeyed, concluding: "Behold, to obey is better than sacrifice."

Samuel continued to chastise Saul and finally told him that because he had rejected the word of the Lord, the Lord had rejected him and he would be king no longer. As Samuel turned to leave, Saul took hold of his mantle and it "rent." It was the perfect example of Saul's contrariness. Samuel turned and told Saul that as the mantle had been rent, so would the Lord tear Saul's king-dom away from him. Samuel then had Agag put to death and both he and Saul returned to their homes. They did not see each other again, but the scripture notes that Samuel "mourned for Saul."

But mourning was not what the Lord wanted. He came to Samuel and chided him for mourning Saul for so long a time and told him to fill his anointing horn with oil and go find Jesse the Bethlehemite. "For," the Lord continued, "I have provided me a king among his sons." Samuel was concerned that if he anointed another king, Saul would kill him, so the Lord said, "Take an heifer with thee, and say, I am come to sacrifice to the Lord." This would provide Samuel with an excuse to find Jesse's chosen son, for he could call Jesse and his sons to the sacrifice and while they were there, he could anoint the next king of Israel. Samuel did what he was told and went to Bethlehem.

An indication of the fear Samuel's presence generated is exem-plified by his arrival in Bethlehem. The elders of the town "trembled at his coming," and asked him, "Comest thou peace-ably?" "Peaceably," Samuel replied. "I am come to sacrifice unto the Lord: sanctify yourselves, and come with me to the sacrifice. And he sanctified Jesse and his sons, and called them to the sacri-fice."

When Samuel saw Eliab, the first of Jesse's sons, he thought he must be looking upon the Lord's anointed, for apparently Eliab was extremely handsome. But the Lord cautioned Samuel not to judge whom the Lord had selected by his height or his counte-nance. "For the Lord seeth not as man seeth; for man looketh on the outward appearance, but the Lord looked on the heart."

Each of Jesse's seven sons passed before Samuel in turn, but he was not inspired to select any of them. Samuel asked Jesse if he had any other sons. Jesse responded that he had one more, but he was with the sheep. Samuel ordered Jesse to send for him. After some time, David, who was "ruddy, and withal of a beautiful coun-tenance," came to see Samuel. "Arise," the Lord said, "anoint him:

for this is he." So Samuel took his horn and anointed David "in the midst of his brethren: and the Spirit of the Lord came upon David from that day forward," but it departed from Saul.

There are two more interesting references to Samuel in the scriptures. They note that he returned home to Ramah and judged Israel all the remainder of his days, going "in circuit" throughout Israel, from Bethel, to Gilgal, to Mizpeh, and to his home in Ramah. When he died, all Israel mourned him. He was buried in his house in Ramah.

The second reference is one of those curious things that is recorded in the scriptures. Saul continued to lead Israel into battle, but the Lord was not with him and Israel was defeated. Then on a certain day the Philistines again came to battle Israel. Saul saw the host and was afraid and trembled. He asked the Lord what he should do. But he received no answer, "neither by dreams, nor by Urim, nor by prophets." So Saul sought out a woman that had a "familiar spirit." She has become known as the *witch of Endor*. Saul disguised himself, went to her, and requested that she bring one back from the dead. Because the practice had been outlawed in Israel on punishment of death and thinking this might be a trap, she was frightened. But after Saul assured her that no harm would come to her, she asked who it was that he wanted her to conjure up. Saul wanted her to bring Samuel back from the dead. The woman complied, "And when [she] saw Samuel, she cried with a loud voice . . . saying, Why has thou deceived me? For thou art Saul."

At first, what the witch of Endor saw was not visible to Saul. When he asked what she had seen, she said it was an old man with a mantle. Saul perceived that it was Samuel and bowed himself to the ground. Samuel asked why Saul had "disquieted" him, and Saul explained his problem: the Lord had left him, there were no dreams, no prophets, and the Philistines were upon him. He wanted to know what he should do.

The answer was not helpful. Samuel reminded Saul of his persistent disobedience and said, "Wherefore then dost thou ask of me, seeing the Lord is departed from thee, and is become thine enemy?" He again reminded Saul that the Lord had "wrested" the kingdom out of his hand and given it to David, because Saul would not obey the Lord's voice. After all this, he told Saul that the Philistines would win the coming battle and that Israel would be defeated. He ended by telling Saul that on the morrow, Saul and his sons would be with him—they would be dead. And it came to pass as Samuel predicted.

The School of the Prophets

circa 1050–640 B.C.
1 Samuel 10:5–12; 19:19–21; 2 Kings 2:3–7, 15–17; 4:38–43; 6:1–7; 22:14; Amos 7:14

Disciples of the prophets were called "sons" in the scriptures, just as teachers and others were sometimes called "father." The title, "School of the Prophets," is not used in the Bible. It was used in the early restoration of the Church when such a school was established to prepare the early brethren to administer the gospel.[83] However, it has always been assumed that the general references in the Bible to "groups" of prophets referred to schools of instruction and worship.

The first reference to these groups of prophets is recorded by Samuel as he prophesied to Saul that he would meet "a company of prophets" with various musical instruments. Samuel continued, stating that Saul would also prophesy and be "turned into another man." All this occurred as Samuel foretold and the proverb went abroad, "Is Saul also among the prophets?"

Such a company of prophets is mentioned with Samuel "standing as appointed over them." Samuel has been accredited as being the founder of the schools for the prophets. It appears that these schools were located in Bethel, in Rama, in Jericho, in Gilgal, and even in Jerusalem. The schools were apparently quite large. In Gilgal a hundred students are spoken of and in Jericho at least

[83] Doctrine & Covenants 88:127–39.

fifty. The scriptures state that the prophetess Huldah was located "in the college" at Jerusalem when she was consulted by the priest, Hilkiah.

There is a very interesting story about one of these groups of prophets that involved Elisha. The group, called "sons of the prophets," informed Elisha that their physical facilities were inadequate, and they want to build larger or additional ones. Elisha agreed and told them to proceed. But they wanted Elisha to accompany them, so he complied. They proceeded to the Jordan River and began cutting timber for construction when one of the axe heads flew off its handle and sank in the river. The worker who had been using the axe was extremely concerned, because it was a borrowed axe. Elisha asked where the head fell, and after being shown the location, cast a stick into the Jordan over the spot. A curious miracle then occurred; the axe head rose to the surface and "swam" to the bank so that it could be retrieved! A story unique in all of scripture.

The scriptures don't indicate how long the schools of the prophets operated. They are only mentioned during the times of Samuel, Elijah, and Elisha. Jezebel tried to destroy all of these schools during the time of Elijah. Obadiah, governor of the king's house at that time, told Elijah that he had saved one hundred of the students by hiding them by fifties in caves.[84] Perhaps Amos' statement that he was neither a prophet nor a prophet's son might indicate that the schools were no longer in operation during his time.

---

[84] 1 Kings 18:3–13.

Nathan

1015 B.C.
2 Samuel 7:1–17; 12; 1 Kings 1; 1 Chronicles 17:1–15; 2 Chronicles 9:29

The name Nathan means *God has given* or *He has given.* Principally, Nathan was a prophet and counselor to David and Solomon.

There are only three events described in detail during Nathan's term as prophet. The first event occurred when David called Nathan to him and stated that he wanted to build a "house" that the Lord could dwell in. The record of that request and the answer is given in both I Samuel and I Chronicles. David had built his own palace and stated that while he lived in a house of cedar, the Ark of God, considered to be the presence of God among them, resided in a house of "curtains," meaning the tabernacle or tent. The word of the Lord came to Nathan and recounted what God had done for Israel and how He had established David as its king, but it would not be David who would build the house of the Lord—it would be his son, Solomon. However, the Lord would be "father" to the son of David, and the son of David would be a "son" to the Lord. He further stated that the Lord's mercy would not depart from him.

The second event involves the chastening of David for his adultery with Bathsheba and the killing of Uriah the Hittite. The story of David and Bathsheba is well-known. While walking on the roof of his house, David saw a woman in her bath. She was "very beautiful to look upon." David inquired after the woman and was told that her name was Bathsheba, the daughter of Eliam and the wife of Uriah the Hittite. David sent messengers to bring Bathsheba to him and eventually, adultery took place. Their union left Bathsheba with child. When she told David of this he sent for Uriah, who was off fighting with the army.

When Uriah came home that evening, David told him to spend time with his wife; but instead, Uriah slept at the door of the king's house. When David asked Uriah why he didn't go home he responded, "The ark, and Israel, and Judah, abide in tents; and my lord Joab, and the servants of my lord, are encamped in the open fields; shall I then go into mine house, to eat and to drink, and to lie with my wife? as thou livest, and as thy soul liveth, I will not do this thing."

David had Uriah tarry another day and gave him food and wine and made him drunk. Uriah spent the night with David's servants, but he still would not go to his house. So the next morning David sent him back to the battle with written instructions to Joab that Uriah be placed in the forefront of the battle, after which the troops were to withdraw. Uriah would be left alone and would undoubtedly be killed. Joab followed these curious instructions and Uriah died.

The rebuke of David by Nathan came in the form of a parable to entrap the king. It was a tale of two men: one was poor with "nothing save one little ewe lamb," the other rich with "many flocks and herds." A banquet was held by the rich man for a visiting traveler. Rather than using an animal from his own extensive flock, the rich man took the poor man's one and only ewe lamb to feed the traveler. David became angry and judged that the rich man should be punished, even that he "should surely die." In addition, the rich man was to restore what was taken fourfold to the poor man, because "he had no pity." Then Nathan told David: "Thou art the man . . . thou hast killed Uriah the Hittite with the sword [of the children of Ammon], and hast taken his wife to be thy wife."

Nathan then pronounced the Lord's judgment upon David: David was doomed to be a violent king for the rest of his life, for as Nathan prophesied, the "sword shall never depart from thine house." In addition, David's "wives" would be defiled in public and the child that Bathsheba had conceived would die. Yet the Lord "put away" the sin of David, and David would not die. Although Bathsheba's first child with David did not survive, their second son became the great King Solomon.

The third event in the scriptures involving Nathan centered around the preservation of David's throne for Solomon. This occurred when David was old and near death. David's son, Adonijah, convinced some of David's leaders that he should be king, and they agreed to follow him. But Nathan and some others declined to do so. Adonijah called together the sons of David (except Solomon) and prepared a banquet preparatory to securing his succession. All this was done without David's knowledge. Nathan, aware that Solomon should be king, spoke to Bathsheba and convinced her that she should gain an audience with David and explain what was afoot. Bathsheba went to David first and then Nathan followed. They told David what Adonijah had done. Nathan then asked David if he wanted Adonijah to be king. David said no. They immediately called for a priest named Zadok, retrieved the "horn of oil" from the tabernacle, and anointed Solomon king of Israel.

These few passages of scripture clearly demonstrate that Nathan was a fearless prophet: blessing when blessings were warranted, rebuking when necessary, and ensuring that the Lord's will was carried out. Perhaps his other acts and further details of his life are not recorded in existing scriptures because they were recorded in his own book, "the book of Nathan the Prophet," one of the books of the Bible that was lost.

Gad the Seer

1031 B.C.
1 Samuel 22:5; 2 Samuel 24:11–19; 1 Chronicles 21:9–19; 29:29; 2 Chronicles 29:25

The name Gad means *good fortune.* He is referred to as both a seer and a prophet in the scriptures, sometimes in the same verse. He was an advisor to King David.

There are only three recorded instances involving Gad in the scriptures. The first is a singular verse noting that he advised David to remove from one location to another while David was hiding from King Saul. When an "evil" spirit came over Saul, David usually soothed him with his harp playing, but Saul had become extremely jealous of David and wanted to kill him because he had been anointed Israel's next king and had become famous throughout all Israel. Hence, David went into hiding and avoided Saul for several years until Saul was killed during a war with the Philistines. It was during this period of hiding that Gad told David to move to a new location in order to preserve his life.

The second time we hear of Gad in the scriptures comes after David "numbered" Israel. He was *not* commanded by the Lord to number the people and in fact, was forbidden to do so; however, he persisted and numbered them anyway. Gad came to him after this and told him that the Lord was displeased and that he would punish all Israel for David's disobedience. The Lord, through Gad, gave David three alternative punishments to choose from: a famine in the land for three years (recorded as seven years in II Samuel), a three-month period when the enemies of Israel would defeat the Israelite armies, or a pestilence that would come upon all the people of Israel. David was reluctant to select from these painful choices and chose to subject himself to the Lord's choice.

The Lord chose the pestilence, and He immediately sent it upon all Israel. The scripture reports that seventy thousand people died. David pled with the Lord and questioned why the people had to suffer for his transgression. As the angel of the Lord was about to destroy Jerusalem with the pestilence, the Lord prevented it and told David (again through Gad) to raise an altar on the thrashing floor of Ornan the Jebusite. David bought the land and built an altar. He placed an offering on the altar and the Lord sent fire to consume it—causing David considerable consternation and fear. At that time the tabernacle was in Gibeon, but at that point, David would not go to Gibeon to offer sacrifices because he was afraid of the angel of destruction after witnessing the consumption of the burnt offering on the thrashing floor of Ornan the Jebusite.

In the third instance, Gad assisted David and Nathan in placing Levites in the temple with musical instruments for use in the sacrificial services.

No other information about Gad the seer is available. Again, mention of him in the scriptures may be limited, perhaps due to the fact that he had written a book of his own, "the book of Gad the Seer," in which he recorded the acts of David. His book is yet another of the lost books of the Bible.

Section III

Divided Israel
The Northern Kingdom

All Israel came together after Solomon's death to make Rehoboam, Solomon's son, the new king. They petitioned Rehoboam to reduce the "heavy yoke" of taxes that Solomon had imposed on them and said if he would, they would follow him. Rehoboam consulted with the old men who had served Solomon and they counseled him to reduce the tax burden and serve the people. Then he consulted the young men he had grown up with and their advice was to make the people's yoke heavier—so it would seem that his "little finger" was thicker than his "father's loins" insofar as taxes were concerned. He took the advice of the younger counselors and, as a result, ten tribes revolted and formed the Kingdom of Israel (or Northern Kingdom) ruled by Jeroboam of the tribe of Ephraim. Rehoboam was left to rule only the tribe of Judah (the Southern Kingdom), which eventually also included the tribe of Benjamin.[85]

---

[85] 1 Kings 12:1–21.

Cameo Appearances by Five Prophets

Ahijah the Shilonite, 956 B.C.
1 Kings 11:28–40; 14:1–18

The name Ahijah means *friend of Jehovah*. There are only two stories that concern Ahijah the Shilonite recorded in the scriptures and both of them involve Jeroboam, the king of Israel.

The first of these took place while Solomon was still alive and king of united Israel. Solomon had made Jeroboam the ruler in charge of the house of Joseph, or the tribes of Ephraim and Manasseh. On one occasion, Jeroboam left Jerusalem clad in a new garment (probably his cloak) and Ahijah followed him. When he found him, Ahijah "caught" the new garment and tore it into twelve pieces. He told Jeroboam to take ten pieces of the cloak: "for thus saith the Lord, the God of Israel, Behold, I will rend the kingdom out of the hand of Solomon, and will give ten tribes to thee." Ahijah was quick to note that the Lord would leave Solomon with one tribe for "Jerusalem's sake," because he had chosen the city out of all Israel. Ahijah declared that the kingdom of Israel would be divided because Solomon had forsaken the Lord and worshiped false gods—Ashtoreth of the Zidonians, Chemosh of the Moabites, and Milcom the god of Ammon—and caused the people to do the same.

Ahijah promised Jeroboam that if he lived the commandments, the Lord would continue his house as ruler of Israel forever. Solomon heard of the call of Jeroboam (although we're not told how) and sought to kill him. Jeroboam left Canaan and went to Egypt until the death of Solomon, after which he became king of the Northern Kingdom.

The second time we hear of Ahijah he is old and blind. The son of Jeroboam was ill and Jeroboam sent his wife (in disguise) to see Ahijah to find out if the child would live. The Lord told Ahijah that Jeroboam's wife was coming and he greeted her before she could assume the disguise of another. Ahijah reminded Jeroboam through his wife that it was the Lord who had placed him on the throne of Israel, and that he would remain king as long as he lived the commandments. But Jeroboam had "done evil above all that were before [him]." He made molten images and worshiped other gods and led the children of Israel astray. Because of this idolatrous worship, none of his kin would assume the kingship after him. Jeroboam's wife was further told that her child would die as soon as she set foot in her house—and it did. But more than this, Ahijah prophesied that the Lord would smite Israel and scatter the people abroad because they had provoked "the Lord to anger," a foreshadowing of the Diaspora to come.

There are no other records of Ahijah the Shilonite.

Iddo the Seer, 961 B.C.
2 Chronicles 9:29; 12:15; 13:22

The name Iddo means *timely* or *lively*. There are but three references to Iddo the Seer in the Old Testament, and all of them refer to records that either he or his contemporaries kept. The first reference indicates that some of the acts of Solomon were kept in the "visions of Iddo the Seer." The book is among the lost books of the Bible. Although no other information is given about the record, the comment indicates that Iddo had multiple visions from the Lord and that they were recorded.

The second reference indicates a book was written by Iddo the Seer concerning genealogies. We have no other information concerning this book. It also is among the lost books of the Bible.

The acts of Abijah, who fought and won battles against King Jeroboam of Israel, are recorded in a third book referred to as "the story of the prophet Iddo." This book is also one of the lost books of the Bible.

No other information is given about this prophet.

Jehu Son of Hanani, 940–914 B.C.
1 Kings 16:1–12; 2 Chronicles 19:2, 3; 20:34

Jehu, whose name means *the living,* was the son of Hanani. He is another prophet that was raised up by the Lord to prophesy condemnation against a king of Israel named Baasha. Baasha committed all of the sins of Jeroboam and so Jehu came and pronounced the Lord's condemnation upon him. The condemnation was very egregious. Like Jeroboam, neither Baasha, nor his house would have posterity. It was prophesied that those of his descendants who died in the cities would have the dogs eat them, while those who died in the country would be eaten by the fowls. Baasha died and was buried and his son Elah reigned over Israel. Two years after he became king, Zimri, captain of half of Elah's chariots, conspired against him. Elah became drunken and Zimri killed him, made himself king, and destroyed all the house of Baasha, including his friends. Thus was the prophecy of Jehu fulfilled.

Jehu also appears approximately thirty years later to both denounce and compliment Jehoshaphat, king of Judah. He denounced him for helping the "ungodly," and because he loved those who hated the Lord. He complimented him for taking away the worship groves of the false gods and preparing his heart to worship the Lord.

Jehu also wrote a book which contained all the acts of Jehoshaphat, but it is one of the lost books of the Bible. No other information is recorded about Jehu the son of Hanani.

Micaiah Son of Imlah, circa 897 B.C.
1 Kings 22:8–38; 2 Chronicles 18

Micaiah, whose name means *who is like God,* was the son of Imlah. He was a prophet during the time Ahab ruled Israel and Jehoshaphat ruled Judah. He may also have lived toward the end of the ministry of Elijah, or just after him.

Ahab had decided to go to war against the king of Syria and invited Jehoshaphat to join him in the war. Jehoshaphat requested that Ahab inquire of the Lord to see if they would prosper. Ahab inquired of his "four hundred" prophets. They said he should go to war and the Lord would deliver Syria into his hands. But Jehoshaphat was not satisfied and asked, "Is there not here a prophet of the Lord besides, that we might inquire of him?" (This is an indication that the four hundred prophets were undoubtedly in one of the schools of the prophets, or false prophets of Ahab, and not prophets "called" of the Lord.) Ahab said yes, and identified Micaiah, the son of Imlah. But he said that he hated him because he only prophesied evil, never good, concerning him.

Micaiah was located by one of Ahab's servants. He was told that Ahab's prophets had prophesied success in the upcoming battle and was advised that he should so prophesy. He was brought before the two kings who sat upon their thrones. At first Micaiah said that Ahab could go up and win the battle, but Ahab, perceiving that he was not telling the truth, did not believe him. He adjured Micaiah to tell the truth about what God had revealed to him. Micaiah then told Ahab of a vision he had had. In it he saw Israel scattered upon the mountains without a shepherd, indicating that the battle would be lost and Ahab would be killed. Ahab became angry because once again Micaiah had prophesied against him. Micaiah continued, saying he had seen the Lord and was informed that the Lord had sent a lying spirit to the prophets of Ahab, after which one of those false prophets struck Micaiah on the cheek. Ahab became wroth and commanded that they take Micaiah to the city and put him in prison until Ahab returned from the battle. But Micaiah again prophesied and told Ahab that if he returned at all from the battle, his (Micaiah's) prophecies were false. The prophet then warned the people that heard him to "harken," or remember what he had said. Ahab went up to the battle and was killed, thus vindicating Micaiah.

Oded the Prophet, 739 B.C.
2 Chronicles 28:5–15

There is only one instance recorded in the scriptures concerning the prophet Oded, whose name means, *restoring.* He appeared after a great battle between Judah and Israel. Israel had won the battle because the Lord was against Judah for worshiping false gods. The army of Israel killed thousands in the battle and took more than two hundred thousand prisoners, including women and children. The prisoners were being taken to Samaria. Normally they would have been made slaves, but Oded appears and counsels them that this would not be acceptable to the Lord because the prisoners were, in fact, their brothers and kindred. Oded tells them that to enslave the prisoners would be as great a sin as those committed by Judah (which sins allowed Israel to be victorious over them in battle). He advises them to let the prisoners return to their homes.

The leadership listened to the prophet. They clothed the prisoners that were naked, fed and "shod" them, and returned them to their families in Jericho. That's all we hear of Oded. He was another of the many prophets who make a cameo appearance in the Bible, but whose appearance testifies to the fact that God was continually working through prophets to guide His chosen people.

Elijah the Tishbite

circa 910 B.C.

1 Kings 17–21; 2 Kings 1–2

Ahab, the son of Omri, was the king in Israel (the Northern Kingdom) before the coming of Elijah. One scripture is very particular when describing this king. It notes that he "did evil in the sight of the Lord," and describes his evil condition as being "above all that were before him." (The scriptures are also very specific when describing the evil of Jeroboam, the first king in the Northern Kingdom.)

To emphasize Ahab's evil ways, it states that although Ahab did all the evil of Jeroboam, those sins were "as if it had been a light thing." Ahab compounded the sins of Jeroboam when he married Jezebel and thereafter worshiped the false god Baal. He built an altar for Baal and a house in Samaria to put the deity in, and he made a "grove" (a specific worship area among trees) where the children of Israel could worship. Finally, it states that "Abab did more to provoke the Lord God of Israel to anger than all the kings of Israel that were before him." It was to this evil king and this state of wickedness that Elijah came. His story is a story of appearances and disappearances, of constantly calling the king and the people to repentance, of signs and miracles, of conflict, and of hiding from Ahab and Jezebel.

Elijah the prophet appears out of nowhere. He's called a Tishbite, but the meaning of that word (or potential location) is uncertain. The name Elijah means, *Jehovah is God,* or *Jehovah is my God.* We know very little about him personally. We do not know his age, who his parents were, or from which tribe in Israel he descended. The only thing we know of his background is that he was "of the inhabitants of Gilead," which was the beautiful hill country east of Jordan. He was a prophet that all Israel revered—and still does. So important was Elijah that Malachi, the last prophet of the Old Testament, prophesied: "Behold, I will send you Elijah the prophet before the coming of the great and dreadful day of the Lord: And he shall turn the heart of the fathers to the children, and the heart of the children to their fathers, lest I come and smite the earth with a curse."[86] Elijah was (and obviously would be in the future) a powerful prophet and a fearless representative of the Lord.

The scriptures introduce Elijah when he informs Ahab that there will be no "dew nor rain" for three and one-half years at his word. In other words, Elijah alone will control the weather. The Lord then tells Elijah to flee immediately and hide "by the brook Cherith." The brook would provide him with water and the Lord "commanded the ravens to feed" him there. Elijah did as he was commanded and there, each morning and each evening, the ravens brought him "bread and flesh," and he drank from the brook. Thus, the ministry of Elijah was not only couched in the constant conflict with Ahab and Jezebel, but in his many miracles.

When the brook Cherith dried up, the Lord commanded Elijah to go to Zarephath where a widow woman would sustain him. As he arrived in Zarephath he saw a woman gathering sticks outside the city gates. Elijah asked for water to drink and "a morsel of bread" to eat. The woman told him of her plight. She had no prepared food. She only had a handful of meal in her barrel and a small amount of oil with which to cook it. She was gathering the sticks to make a fire, bake what was left of the food, feed herself and her son, and then die.

---

[86] Malachi 4:5, 6.

Elijah told the widow to proceed— to bake the cake but to give it to him—then bake one for herself and her son. He promised her that the barrel would not "waste," meaning it would not go empty, and that the oil would not "fail," or run out, until the rains came again. And the miracle occurred. Neither the barrel nor the oil reduced during Elijah's stay.

The woman's son, however, eventually became ill and died, and she railed on Elijah. "What have I to do with thee, O thou man of God? art thou come unto me to call my sin to remembrance, and to slay my son?" But Elijah had compassion on the woman. He carried her son up to the loft of the house and placed him on his own bed. He prayed and asked an interesting question of the Lord: ". . . hast thou also brought evil upon the widow with whom I sojourn, by slaying her son?" Then Elijah "stretched" (laid) upon the child three times and prayed that the Lord would restore the soul to the child. The Lord heard his cry and the child revived. Elijah took the child to his mother and the woman confessed that, "Now by this I know that thou art a man of God."

The Lord next commanded Elijah to return to Ahab. The drought had lasted for more than three years and the famine was "sore." Ahab called for Obadiah, the governor of his house, and told him they were going to take the royal horses and mules and find grass for them. (We're told that Obadiah "feared" the Lord and that when Jezebel tried to kill all the prophets, Obadiah had saved the lives of a hundred of them by hiding them in caves and feeding them. These prophets were undoubtedly members of the schools of the prophets first begun during Samuel's ministry.)

Obadiah and Ahab split up as they looked for pasture. As Obadiah searched, he met Elijah. He "fell on his face" and asked Elijah if it was truly he. Elijah answered that it was, and told Obadiah to go and tell Ahab where he was—in spite of the fact that Elijah had hidden from Ahab and Jezebel for more than three years.

Obadiah was fearful for his life. He thought if he told Ahab that Elijah would meet him that Elijah would just disappear—be carried away by the "Spirit of the Lord." He reminded Elijah that Ahab had been searching everywhere for him—even searching through adjacent nations—and when the leaders of those nations had told Ahab that Elijah was not there, he had extracted an oath from them to that effect, implying that they could expect retribution from him if Elijah were later found on their soil. Obadiah also reminded Elijah that he had even saved some of the prophets. To calm Obadiah's fears Elijah assured him that he would meet with Ahab, and Obadiah left to inform Ahab of the meeting.

When Ahab finally confronts Elijah, his first words are haughty and filled with disdain. "Art thou he that troubleth Israel?" But Elijah would have none of that and succinctly clarified that it was Ahab and his house that had caused Israel's troubles, because they had "forsaken the commandments of the Lord . . . and followed Baalim." It's obvious that Elijah has been instructed in what he should do thereafter because he immediately told Ahab to call "all Israel" to Mt. Carmel where an altar to the Lord was once located. He also instructed Ahab to call the four hundred and fifty prophets of Baal (and the four hundred prophets of the groves that Jezebel had been supporting all this time) to meet him at the altar. After the people and the false prophets gather, Elijah prepares for what becomes a contest between the god Baal, and the God of Israel—and the people agree to follow whichever deity wins.

Two altars were to be built and the sacrifices prepared, but no fire would be kindled. It was agreed that the true God would send down fire to consume the sacrifice, and the people responded to these terms by stating, "It is well spoken."

Baal's prophets went first. They prepared the altar and the sacrifice and began calling upon their god. But nothing happened, and Elijah mocked them. "Cry aloud," he said. "For he is a god; either he is talking, or he is pursuing, or he is in a journey, or peradventure he sleepeth, and must be awaked"! And in the manner of their worship, the scripture reports that they "cried aloud, and cut themselves . . . with knives and lancets, till the blood gushed out upon them." But still nothing happened.

Then it was Elijah's turn. He repaired the altar of the Lord with twelve stones, one for each of the tribes of Israel, and had a deep trench dug around it. Then he stacked wood on the altar and placed the sacrifice upon it. Finally, to add insult to injury he poured water over the sacrifice: one time, and then a second, and a third until the trench was full. Then Elijah called upon God to show the people that He was the God of Israel. The Lord immediately sent fire from heaven and consumed the sacrifice—the wood—the stones—the dust—and "licked up the water that was in the trench." The people fell on their faces and worshiped! Then Elijah instructed them to destroy the wicked prophets of Baal—which they did.

After the contest, Elijah told Ahab to eat and drink in celebration for the sound of rain was coming. Then he told his servant to go look toward the sea, anticipating a storm—but the servant saw nothing and reported it to Elijah. Six more times he went to search the skies, but always he returned with the same discouraging report. Then on the seventh time, he reported that he saw a little cloud over the sea. Elijah commanded Ahab to get to his chariot, for the rain was coming. The heavens turned black, the wind blew, and "there was a great rain."

Ahab sped in his chariot to his palace in Jezreel, and a most unique verse occurs at this point in the scriptures. It states that "the hand of the Lord was on Elijah;" that he girded up his loins (meaning that he tied his robes up) and "ran" faster than Ahab could drive his chariot, and arrived at the entrance of Jezreel before Ahab. A most interesting miracle.

When Ahab arrived in Jezreel, he immediately went to Jezebel and told her all that had occurred. She was enraged and sent a message to Elijah that she would kill him before the end of the next day. Again Elijah fled. He traveled a day's journey into the wilderness beyond Beersheba, sat under a juniper tree, and lamented. "Take away my life," he moaned. But the Lord would have none of that. An angel was sent to Elijah. It touched him and commanded, "Arise and eat." We're not told what food was provided nor how it was provided, but Elijah ate and drank. Again the angel commanded him to eat, because he was to take a long journey. Elijah ate again and departed on his journey. While on the journey, he ate nothing for the forty days and nights it took him to get to Mount Horeb—the mountain of Moses and the ten commandments. When he arrived on the mount, Elijah rested in a cave. There the word of the Lord came to him and asked, "What doest thou here, Elijah?" Elijah, still somewhat despondent, responded ". . . the children of Israel have forsaken thy covenant, thrown down thine altars, and slain thy prophets with the sword; and I, even I only, am left; and they seek my life, to take it away."

Then the Lord spoke to Elijah and said, "Go forth, and stand upon the mount before the Lord." A great wind came and rent the mountains and broke the rocks—but the Lord was not in the wind. Then an earthquake occurred—but the Lord was not in the earthquake. After the earthquake came a fire—but the Lord was not in the fire. Then there came a "still small voice." And when Elijah heard it, he wrapped himself in his mantle and stood at the entrance of the cave, and once again the Lord asked, "What doest thou here, Elijah?" And again Elijah responded that the children of Israel were seeking his life.

The Lord spoke to Elijah giving him three assignments: first he was to go "anoint Hazael to be king over Syria;" second, he was to anoint "Jehu the son of Nimshi," to be king over Israel; and third, he was to anoint Elisha to succeed him as prophet. And then, as if to console him, the Lord told Elijah that he was not alone, that there were seven thousand righteous souls left in Israel. This is perhaps a symbolic number to indicate that there were yet others in Israel beside Elijah who followed the commandments of the Lord.

Elijah left the mount and found Elisha plowing in a field with "twelve yoke of oxen before him, and he was with the twelfth." Elijah "cast his mantle" upon Elisha, which was the symbol of his call to follow him. It is from this experience that we gain the saying, he has the mantle of authority or the mantle of his office.

Elisha prepared a meal for his parents, said goodbye, and followed Elijah.

✦ ✦ ✦

Elijah's ministry jumps from one event to another at this point. The next episode concerns the story of Naboth, a resident of Jerusalem. Naboth had a vineyard that Ahab coveted. Ahab offered to buy it, but Naboth refused because it was the inheritance he had received from his fathers under the Law of Moses. Ahab fell into depression and pouted like a child; he laid upon his bed, turned his face away (presumably to the wall), and would not eat. Jezebel discovered the problem and through lying and deceit accused Naboth of blasphemy, convicted him, and had him stoned. Jezebel told Ahab what had occurred, and he immediately arose and took possession of the vineyard. But the Lord told Elijah about this injustice. He went to Ahab and told him that as the dogs had licked the blood of Naboth, so also would they lick Ahab's blood. And as for Jezebel? The dogs would "eat Jezebel by the wall of Jezreel."

Although Ahab had already seen the prophecies of Elijah fulfilled for years, with this prophecy he finally got the message. Ahab repented! He rent his clothes, put on sackcloth, and fasted. The word of the Lord came to Elijah and told him that "Ahab humbleth himself." Therefore, He would not bring "evil in [Ahab's] days, but in his son's days." Three years went by without war. Then war came again and the prophecies of Elijah were fulfilled. Ahab was slain in battle and his blood spilled on his chariot. The chariot was washed in a pool of water in Samaria and the dogs licked the water mixed with blood. Later, Jezebel was thrown from a tower window at Jezreel, trampled by a chariot, and killed. When they went to bury her the next day, the wild dogs had already been there and they only found her skull and the palms of her hands.[87]

When next we hear of Elijah, he is calling Ahaziah, Ahab's successor, to repentance. Ahaziah had suffered an injury from a

[87] 2 Kings 9.

fall through a lattice. He had sent messengers to discern from the god Baalzebub of Ekron whether he would live or die of his injury. Elijah heard of it and asked the messengers why Ahaziah had sent his inquiry to a false god who could not prevent Ekron's military defeat rather than to the true God of Israel. He pronounced that because Ahaziah had done this thing, he would die. The messengers returned and told the king what Elijah had said. The king asked what kind of man it was that told them this. They responded that he was "an hairy man, and girt with a girdle of leather about his loins." The description convinced the king that it was Elijah. Ahaziah then sent solders to fetch Elijah, and Elijah performed the following bizarre group of miracles. A contingent comprising a captain and fifty soldiers confronted Elijah and told him that the king wanted him. Elijah commanded fire to come down from heaven to consume the captain and his fifty—and it did. Ahaziah sent another captain and fifty—with the same result. A third was sent, but obviously the captain had heard of the prior two disastrous incidents and bowed himself before Elijah and pled for his life and the lives of his men. His plea was granted. Then the angel of the Lord commanded Elijah to go with the captain and "be not afraid of him." So Elijah went with the captain to confront Ahaziah and deliver the Lord's message: "Forasmuch as thou hast sent messengers to inquire of Baalzebub the god of Ekron . . . thou shalt not come down off that bed on which thou art gone up, but shalt surely die." And thus Ahaziah died, "according to the word of the Lord which Elijah had spoken."

The last event in Elijah's life involves the Lord taking him to heaven in a whirlwind. The Lord had sent Elijah to Bethel, and Elijah said to Elisha," Tarry here, I pray thee; for the Lord hath sent me to Bethel." But Elisha would not be left behind and said to Elijah, "As the Lord liveth, and as thy soul liveth, I will not leave thee." So they went to Bethel together. Twice more Elijah told Elisha to "tarry," once because Elijah was to go to Jericho and then to the Jordan River—and twice Elisha refused. Finally, at the banks of the Jordan, Elijah took his mantle and smote the waters of Jordan—and they parted so that he and Elisha could cross on dry ground. Elisha had become Elijah's symbolic son and as the firstborn under the Law of Moses, he was entitled to a "double portion" of his "father's" possessions. And so Elisha requested that of Elijah, which in Elijah's case would be a "double portion" of his spirit, or the power he held. Elijah (knowing what was about to happen) said he had asked for a hard thing, but if Elisha saw him when he departed it would be so, and if he did not see him, it would not. They continued walking and before long there "appeared a chariot of fire, and horses of fire." They came between Elijah and Elisha, separating them, and Elijah was caught "up by a whirlwind into heaven." "And Elisha saw it, and he cried, My father, my father, the chariot of Israel, and the horsemen thereof. And he saw him no more."

There is one other reference to Elijah's activities in the Old Testament. In Chronicles we read of a letter that he sent to King Jehoram of Judah (son of Jehoshaphat) in which he condemned the king. Jehoram had killed his own brothers to gain the throne and committed the sins of Ahab, king of Israel. Because of his wickedness, Elijah prophesied that a plague would come from the Lord and smite the people, including Jehoram's children, his wives, and his goods. Jehoram himself would succumb to a sickness of the bowels—"until thy bowels fall out." Jehoram's reign began very near the translation of Elijah, and possibly before the death of Jehoram's father, Jehoshaphat;[88] therefore, the aged Elijah must have left a message for the king before he was translated that was possibly delivered to the king after Elijah's translation.

In the New Testament, Elijah (called Elias) appeared on the Mount of Transfiguration with Moses when the Savior was transfigured.[89] John the Baptist is foreshadowed as coming in the spirit

---

[88] 2 Kings 8:16.
[89] Matthew 17:3.
[90] Luke 1:17.

and power of Elias.[90] And there are multiple other references to Elijah throughout the New Testament.[91]

Other than the Old Testament letter to Jehoram, however, there are no written works of Elijah. But while his recorded words and deeds are few, they are exceptional. His condemnation of evil was specific and unrelenting. His miracles were explicit and magnificent. His impression upon the Israelites was only surpassed by that of Moses. But Elijah's legacy has been enlarged by the Jews' unrelenting belief that he will yet return and restore the kingdom to them. Each year at Passover the Jews traditionally set a place for him at their tables and leave their doors ajar so that he can return and dine with them.

That return—so longed for by the Jews—was fulfilled during the Restoration in the latter days when Elijah appeared to Joseph Smith and Oliver Cowdery in the Kirtland Temple and restored the keys of the sealing power of the priesthood, in fulfillment of the prophecy of Malachi.[92]

[91] Matthew 16:14; 27:47–49; Mark 6:14, 15; 9:4;   [92] Doctrine & Covenants 110:13–16.
15:35, 36; Luke 4:25, 26; 9: 30; James 5:17.

Elisha

circa 900 B.C.
1 Kings 19:16–21; 2 Kings 2–13

Elisha was the disciple of Elijah, called to follow Elijah while Elisha was plowing the fields with oxen, and he eventually became the successor to Elijah in the office of prophet. His name means *God of or is salvation,* or *God shall save.* We hear little of Elisha after his call until Elijah is taken up into heaven in a chariot of fire. Elisha watched the translation of Elijah and received the mantle of Elijah as the sign that he had been blessed with Elijah's calling—his mantle of authority. He returned from the wilderness after Elijah's translation and, as though to test his prophetic call, struck the Jordan River with Elijah's mantle. The river parted as it had for Elijah, and he crossed over on dry ground. The "sons of the prophets" who had been watching the proceedings bowed down to Elisha, acknowledging his call.

Elisha was the prophet to Israel through the reigns of Jehoram, Jehu, Jehoahaz, and Joash. He stood in sharp contrast to Elijah (a wild man of the desert who sought isolation in the wilderness) since he preferred city life. While Elijah was constantly hiding and appearing, Elisha was available to all. He was a prophet who performed a veritable multitude of miracles.

The first of his many miracles occurred in Jericho. The city's springs had become polluted and the sons of the prophets petitioned him for help. He called for a "cruse," placed salt in it, went to the head of the spring, and cast the salt into it with the blessing that it would heal the waters. It did.

One day Elisha was traveling from Jericho to Bethel (one of many travels in the area). He must have been a bald man for while he traveled, a group of "children" came out and "mocked" him crying, "Go up, thou bald head; go up, thou bald head." The mockery must have been more than just children's play because Elisha cursed them in the name of the Lord. The curse and the punishment for their actions were fulfilled when two she bears came out of the woods, attacked the children, and "tare forty and two . . . of them."

Next Elisha provided water for the kings of Israel, Judah, and Edom in their unified battle against the king of Moab. At his command, the valley they were fighting in became full of "ditches." Without wind or rain but by the word of the Lord, he filled the ditches with water so that the armies and their beasts could drink. The opposing army of Moab saw the glowing reflection of the sun on the water and thought it was blood on the ground as a result of the three kings fighting each other. They attacked, were beaten severely, and fled.

Many of the miracles that Elisha performed were personal—miracles that helped individuals in need. One such miracle was for a poor widow, one of the wives of the sons of the prophets. Her husband had died and left her in debt. She pled with Elisha to help her lest they take her two sons to be bondsmen. Her only asset was a pot of oil. Elisha told her to borrow as many pots as she could. With the pots in her possession, Elisha told her to pour from her pot of oil into the many pots, and she did until all of the pots were full. Now she could sell the oil and pay her debts.

Elisha did circuits from city to city, undoubtedly teaching in the schools of the prophets that were in them. On each circuit he passed through Shunem. He was recognized by a woman there and she persuaded her husband to prepare a room for him so that each time he passed by he could rest and refresh himself. She also fed him when he lodged there. After some time, Elisha told his servant, Gehazi, to call the Shunammite woman to him and when she arrived, he asked what she would have him do for her to repay her hospitality. She did not ask Elisha for anything, but Gehazi told Elisha that she had no son and that her husband was old. Elisha summoned the woman and promised her a son the next year. The woman's interesting response was, "Nay, my lord, thou man of God, do not lie unto thine handmaid." But the child came.

As the story is told, when the child had grown, he fell and hit his head. He was taken to his mother and "he sat on her knees till noon, and then died. And she went up, and laid him on the bed of the man of God, and shut the door upon him, and went out." Then she went to find Elisha. When she found him, she "caught him by the feet." Gehazi attempted to remove her, but Elisha told him to leave her alone because she was "vexed within her." He explained to Gehazi that the Lord had hidden the woman's problem from him. After learning from the distraught mother that her child was dead, Elisha sent Gehazi with his staff to place it "upon the face of the child." Gehazi did as he was instructed but nothing happened. Elisha then proceeded to the house and "lay upon the child." The scripture is very descriptive, stating that he "put his mouth upon his mouth, and his eyes upon his eyes, and his hands upon his hands: and he stretched himself upon the child; and the flesh of the child waxed warm." Elisha paused and paced back and forth. He again put himself upon the child, "and the child sneezed seven times, and . . . opened his eyes." Then he returned the child to the grateful mother.

Elisha returned to Gilgal where there was another school of the prophets. They prepared a large meal in honor of Elisha but while gathering the ingredients, they accidently put poisonous herbs into the pot. Upon eating they discovered that "there [was] death in the pot." Elijah cast some "meal" into the pot and "healed" it so that no one became ill or died. On another occasion he was brought some bread to eat, twenty loaves of barley and ears of corn. He told them to share the food with the people around him, but they answered that there was not enough for the hundred men that were there. Elisha again instructed them to feed the people, for "thus saith the Lord, They shall eat, and shall leave thereof." All were fed, and there was food left over.

One of the great miracles Elisha performed involved a man named Naaman, captain of the armies of Syria. He was reportedly a great and honorable man, but he had leprosy. A maid servant to his wife told her that leprosy could be healed in Israel, so the king of Syria sent a letter to the king of Israel requesting that Naaman be healed. The king of Israel "rent his clothes," a common response to perceived catastrophic events in Old Testament times. Elisha heard of the situation and told the king to send Naaman to him so that Naaman would know there was a prophet in Israel.

Naaman and his entourage soon arrived at the door of Elisha's house. Elisha didn't even go out to greet him, but instead sent Gehazi with a note telling Naaman to go bathe in the Jordan River seven times. Naaman, expecting some great thing to be required of him, became angry. "Are not Abana and Pharpar, rivers of Damascus, better than all the waters of Israel? may I not wash in them, and be clean?" And he turned and left Elisha's house in a rage.

Then another servant spoke to him calmly and said, my lord, "if the prophet had bid thee do some great thing, wouldest thou not have done it?" And he convinced Naaman to try the simple thing Elisha had required of him. So Naaman humbled himself and bathed in the Jordan River seven times—and became clean. Afterwards, Naaman returned to Elisha and offered him a reward for his services, but Elisha refused Naaman's offer. However Gehazi, Elisha's servant, could not pass up a good thing. He caught up with Naaman and asked for "a talent of silver, and two changes of garments," using the ruse that Elisha had asked him to obtain these goods for "two young men of the sons of the prophets." Naaman gave him what he asked for and more, but when Elisha discovered what Gehazi had done, he cast the leprosy of Naaman upon Gehazi and upon his "seed" forever. And Gehazi left the presence of Elisha a leper, "as white as snow."

Elisha was constantly involved with the sons or schools of the prophets. On one occasion they asked him to allow them to build a new and larger lodging for themselves and him. Elisha agreed and told them to go ahead. They petitioned him to go with them and he followed them to the banks of the Jordan River to cut trees. As noted in this same story about the Schools of the Prophets, as the cutting progressed, the axe head used by one of the workers came off and dropped into the river. The worker became distraught because the axe had been borrowed. Elisha asked where the axe had entered the river and the worker pointed to the place. Elisha cut a stick and tossed it into the river over the spot. The axe head rose to the surface and "did swim" to the shore where it could be retrieved by the worker! A most unique miracle.

On another occasion the army of the king of Syria was confronting the armies of the king of Israel, but the Israelites seemed to anticipate the Syrians' every move. The king asked his advisors to find the traitor in their midst. They told him it was not one of them, but Elisha the prophet who was revealing the movements of the Syrian army to the leaders of the Israelites. The king, finding out that Elisha was at Dothan, sent chariots and a "great host" to fetch him. They encompassed the city and Elisha's servant became extremely concerned. Elisha was calm and told the servant, "they that be with us are more than they that be with them." Elisha prayed that the eyes of his servant would be opened so he could see what Elisha saw, and when they were, the servant saw that "the mountain was full of horses and chariots of fire round about Elisha." Elisha caused the men of the Syrian army to become blind. He then led them to Samaria and after restoring their vision, released them. When the king of Israel saw how vulnerable the Syrians were at that point, he asked Elisha if they should "smite" them.

But Elisha said no, and asked the king if he would smite those whom he had taken captive with the sword. Instead, they fed the Syrians and let them return to their master. "So the bands of Syria came no more into the land of Israel" at that time. (But later, Benhadad, king of Syria, gathered all his host and again besieged Samaria.)

There was a great famine in Samaria at this time. The famine persisted and became so bad that "an ass's head was sold for fourscore pieces of silver." People were even eating their own children. But in spite of all this, Elisha prophesied that there would be incredible plenty in Samaria.

During the famine, four leprous men sat at the gate of the Samarian city that was under siege. After some discussion, they concluded that it would be better to take their chances with the Syrians than to remain in the city and die of famine. However, when they reached the camp of the Syrians, no one was there: "For the Lord had made the host of the Syrians to hear a noise of chariots, and a noise of horses, even the noise of a great host: and they said to one another, Lo, the king of Israel hath hired against us the kings of the Hittites, and the kings of the Egyptians, to come upon us." Therefore, the Syrian soldiers rose "in the twilight" and fled for their lives, leaving their tents, their horses, and all their possessions and supplies behind them. The people immediately went out and "spoiled" the Syrian camp and Elisha's prophecy was fulfilled. The deserted supplies fulfilled all their needs—and more.

Elisha was heavily involved with governments. He fulfilled the assignment of Elijah by anointing Hazael king of Syria and assigning an unnamed child of the prophets (another member of the school of the prophets) to take a box of oil, go to Ramothgilead, and anoint Jehu king of Israel. Jehu was the king that eventually destroyed the house of Ahab and witnessed the death of Jezebel, again fulfilling the prophecies of Elijah. On Elisha's deathbed (from some unidentified sickness), Joash, king of Israel, came to him weeping. Joash was a good king and had tried to destroy the worship of Baal and restore the commandments of God to the Northern Kingdom, but he had constantly fought wars with Syria. From his deathbed, Elisha told him to take his bow and shoot an arrow eastward, then beat the remaining arrows on the ground. The king did, but he only beat upon the ground three times. Elisha was angry. He told the king that he should have smitten the ground five or six times because the arrows signified the number of times Joash would defeat the Syrians. Now, rather than consuming the Syrians, he would only be victorious three times.

Elisha died of his sickness and was buried, but the great ministry of miracles that comprised his life was not over. There was as yet one more miracle to come, even after his death. A group was carrying a man to be buried when they spotted a band of men thought to be Moabites invading Israel. Hastily, they "cast" the body of the man into the sepulcher of Elisha and fled. But when the body of the dead man "touched the bones of Elisha, he revived, and stood up on his feet." Another very astonishing miracle.

Elisha ministered as a prophet in Israel for more than forty-five years. He was warmhearted and generous. He was courageous, a diplomat, and a statesman. He could be severe and stern, but only when the occasion demanded it. He was a great teacher, and served as a confidant to kings who addressed him as "father" and themselves as his "sons." When illness took his life, Joash, the king of Israel, "came down unto him, and wept over his face, and said, O my father, my father, the chariot of Israel, and the horsemen thereof," indicating the great esteem the leaders of Israel had for Elisha.

Jonah

circa 820–793 B.C.
2 Kings 14:23–25; Book of Jonah; Matthew 12:38–41; 16:4; Luke 11:29, 30

The prophet Jonah (whose name means *dove*) was the son of Amittai. He lived in Gathhepher, which was a town on the border of Zebulun.

Jonah lived during or before the reign of Jeroboam II of the Northern Kingdom—between 820 B.C. and 793 B.C. The time of his ministry seems to coincide with that of Amos and Hosea. Other than the book of Jonah itself, there is only one other scriptural reference that refers to his ministry. It confirms the fulfillment of a prophecy that Jonah made. Apparently he prophesied that Jeroboam II would reclaim portions of the original coast of Israel from its enemies, which was accomplished.[93] Only this summary of the prophecy and its conclusion is given. However, even though this reference is limited, it indicates that Jonah was active as a prophet before the experiences recorded in his book, even though we do not have those records today.

The book of Jonah begins when the Lord instructed him to go to Nineveh and call the people of that city to repentance. Jonah is fearful. He shrinks from the call and instead of going to Nineveh, he travels to Joppa where he boards a ship for Tarshish. From there the story of Jonah is familiar. The Lord causes a storm to

---

[93] 2 Kings 14:25; Josephus: Antiquities 9.10.1.

arise and while Jonah is asleep in the hold, the Gentile sailors all pray to their gods to be saved from the wind and the violent waves. When he is awakened by the captain of the ship, Jonah admits that he is the cause of the storm and instructs the captain to throw him into the sea so that the storm will abate. The Gentile captain paused only a moment, then tossed Jonah into the sea. The sea immediately became calm.

In the meantime, the Lord had prepared a great fish to swallow Jonah and after three days in the belly of this fish, it vomits Jonah onto the shore—per the Lord's instructions. (The cooperating fish in this venture remains unidentified.) The Lord then tells Jonah a second time to go to Nineveh and call the people to repentance. Jonah is now convinced that he must obey, and he goes to Nineveh.

Nineveh is described as a "great city" because it took three days to cross it on foot. Jonah entered into the city a distance of one day's distance and prophesied that in forty days the Lord would destroy it. Fortunately for the people, they "believed God"—every one of them. They all repented and fasted and prayed, including the king. So God changed his mind and did not destroy Nineveh after all.

Jonah angrily left the city, complaining to the Lord that after all he had been through that it would have been better for him "to die than to live." He built a booth to sit in and waited in the hot sun to see what would happen to the city. From all appearances, Jonah didn't want the city to repent any more than he wanted to go there and call it to repentance in the first place.

The Lord prepared a "gourd" during the night to shade Jonah from the sun while he waited to see what the Lord would do, and the scripture notes that he was "exceeding glad" for the gourd. But the Lord was teaching Jonah a lesson. He prepared a "worm" that destroyed the gourd during the second night and when Jonah arose the next morning the gourd was dead. However, the Lord was not through with Jonah yet. He caused a "vehement east wind" to blow and Jonah, now shadeless, had to contend with the hot sun *and* the hot wind. Jonah again complained and told the Lord, "It is better for me to die than to live." The Lord then concluded the lesson He was trying to teach Jonah. He chided him for complaining about the gourd because he did not labor for it, nor help it grow. He told Jonah that more than 120,000 people in Nineveh had repented, but as yet they could not "discern between their right hand and their left hand," a descriptive analogy informing us that they didn't even know the God who had spared them.

On the surface, the story of Jonah only seems to be a story about a reluctant prophet and a forgiving God; however, it also contains a foreshadowing of the death, burial, and resurrection of Jesus. Upon multiple occasions the leadership of the Jews asked Jesus to show them a sign. They did not mean the multiple signs he was giving them through his many miracles, but the sign of the coming of the Son of Man. They could not receive that sign because it was reserved for a future time, so the Lord told them the only sign they would receive would be the sign of the prophet Jonas (Jonah). Jonah was "buried" in the belly of a great fish for three days—the body of the Lord would be in the tomb for three days. After the third day, Jonah came forth from the belly of the fish—just as the Lord rose from the tomb (the symbolic "belly" of the earth) after the third day.

The four chapters of the book of Jonah seem to be written in parallel halves: Chapters 1 and 2; then 3 and 4. Each contains a call from God and an answer from Jonah (1:1–3; 3:1–3). Each recites Jonah's encounter with Gentiles who are forced to consider God's influence and power (1:4–11; 3:4–11). Each records Jonah's attitude (which causes Jonah to have a confrontation with God) (1:12–17; 4:1–9). And finally, each records God's forgiveness and compassionate deliverance (2:1–9; 4:10–12).

Nothing is known of the time or manner of Jonah's death.

Amos

circa 808–740 B.C.
Book of Amos

Amos—whose name means *burden*—ministered in the days of King Uzziah of Judah (about 740 B.C.) and King Jeroboam II of Israel (about 750 B.C.), even though his book describes events prior to the reign of those kings. He notes that he was a shepherd and a native of Tekoa, which was near Bethlehem. According to the scriptures, his ministry began two years before "the earthquake." He doesn't elaborate on this earthquake although it must have been very powerful since Zechariah also references it[94] when he compares it to an earthquake he prophesies will occur prior to the Second Coming.

The book of Amos warns the people that the Lord is angry because they're indulging in the extravagance of luxury, worshiping of false gods, and neglecting the God of Israel. God condemned the sins of both the Northern and Southern Kingdoms and emphasized that he would do "nothing, but he revealeth his secret unto his servants the prophets." He warned the people that He would not only punish the people of the two kingdoms for their sins, but also the kings of those kingdoms because they had led the people astray. And since they would not repent, he warned the people of the Northern Kingdom that they would "surely be

---

[94] Zechariah 14:5.

led away captive out of their own land," and their king, Jeroboam II, would be slain by the sword.

Because of the great wickedness of both kingdoms, Amos envisioned the day when the Lord would "send a famine in the land." It would not be a famine of food or water, but of "hearing the words of the Lord." He also prophesied that the Israelites would be scattered among all nations, but would eventually be gathered back to their own land (a prophecy that has been partially fulfilled with the establishment of the State of Israel for the Jews.)

Amos saw five visions in all. As a result, he prophesied of the judgments that would befall the various nations surrounding the promised land. His most notable prophecies, however, regarded the judgments that would befall Judah and Israel and their leaders. He frequently alluded to natural objects and agricultural occupations in his prophecies, perhaps a natural way of expressing himself since he had spent his early life had been as a herdsman.

Nothing is known of the time or manner of his death.

Hosea

784–725 B.C.
Book of Hosea

osea was the son of Beeri. His name may mean *Jehovah is help* or *salvation*. Hosea was a prophet to the Northern Kingdom of Israel. He is generally thought to be the only prophet to the Northern Kingdom who left a written record of his prophecies. His ministry was long, identified because of the kings he lived under: Uzziah, Jotham, Ahaz, and Hezekiah, kings of Judah; and Jeroboam II in Israel. He served as a prophet for approximately fifty-nine years, between 784–725 B.C.

Hosea's first prophecy came as a result of his marriage to a "wife of whoredoms," and their ensuing child. His marriage was a similitude of the "marriage" covenant between God and Israel. Because Israel had sinned, it had broken the covenant with God and as a result, the Northern Kingdom would go into captivity.

The sins of the Kingdom of Israel were threefold: (1) there was no truth among the inhabitants; (2) they had no mercy; and (3) they had rejected the knowledge of God. Because they had rejected that knowledge, the Lord said He would reject them and disperse them. It appears from Hosea's writings that even though those in the Northern Kingdom were worshiping false gods, they continued to perform the requirements of the Law of Moses—although without the proper spirit.

Hosea continues his prophecy by also condemning the sins of Judah. Its people would be conquered, removed from the prom-

d land, then returned to the promised land, only to eventually
persed again. Yet even in their diaspora, Judah would be
ved, and eventually the two kingdoms would again be one.
sea's book is a constant reminder of the relationship be-
the reproach for sin, the resultant punishment, and the received upon repenting and returning to God. He takes the
time in his book to enumerate long lists of sins, both of the people
and of the leaders, and through the words of the Lord, he chastens
them. Even though he declares captivity as the general punishment for both kingdoms, he laments the sinful condition of both
kingdoms and promises that eventually the Lord will reclaim them.

One of the great teachings of Hosea is that God loves his people
even though he chastises and punishes them. This theme is carried throughout his entire book. Hosea concludes that the people
brought the punishments of God upon themselves by their own
actions, but God's goodness will eventually prevail and His love
will "heal their backsliding." He prophesied that the eventual
dispersion of both kingdoms and all the tribes would continue
until the final gathering before the Second Coming.

Besides his book, there are no other references to Hosea.

Six Unnamed Prophets

This chapter describes six unnamed prophets that appear, deliver their message or deal with the circumstances at hand, then disappear from the text. They existed at different times as indicated by the dates identified by each story. They are dealt with together in this chapter rather than chronologically and in individual chapters because of the limited historical detail concerning their lives.

A Man of God, circa 1050 B.C.
1 Samuel 2:27–36

The first of the unnamed prophets enters the Old Testament at the time of Eli and the boy Samuel. Eli was the high priest in Israel during this period. His sons, Hophni and Phinehas, were officiating priests and Eli intended for them to judge Israel after he died. But they were wicked— extracting gifts from those who came to offer sacrifice and cavorting with the women who came to the doors of the tabernacle. Eli was told by the Lord to correct them, and although he chastised them, he did not relieve them of their duties—and they didn't stop sinning. As a result, an unnamed "man of God" came to Eli. The man of God reminded Eli that his predecessors had been chosen to officiate in the priestly offices from the time of the Exodus forward. Although it had been the Lord's intention to maintain that line continuously, wickedness on the part of those destined for such calls caused them to be "lightly esteemed" by the Lord. He would now select only those who honored Him.

Finally the man of God prophesied that Eli's sons would be cut off "in the flower of their age." As a sign, the man of God bluntly prophesied that both of Eli's sons would die "in one day." The prophecy was fulfilled when the Philistines defeated the army of Israel and captured the Ark of the Covenant, killing both sons in the process.[95]

Prophets Sent to Manasseh, King of Judah, circa 698–642 B.C.
2 Kings 21:10–18; 2 Chronicles 33:1–18.

In the Second book of Kings it indicates that God sent His servants, the prophets, to Manasseh, king of Judah. Manasseh began his reign when he was twelve years old and reigned for fifty-five years. In Kings, God condemned Manasseh for the evil he had done, which in turn caused the people of Judah to sin. Those sins are recorded as being great, like the abominations of the heathen God had cast out of the land of promise. Manasseh built altars for Baalim, worshiped the host of heaven (meaning the sun, moon, and stars), and built altars for them in God's Temple. He sacrificed children, used enchantments, and was involved with witchcraft and wizards.

At this point, the writer of Chronicles indicates the Lord spoke to Manasseh and the people, but they did "not harken" to His words. He sent several unidentified prophets to them who prophesied that because of their wickedness, the Lord would bring "evil"

Prophets of the Old Testament

---

[95] 1 Samuel 4:1–11.

upon both Jerusalem and Judah. The evil would be so great that those who heard about it would have "both [their] ears . . . tingle." The Chronicles report that the king of Assyria eventually captured Jerusalem and defeated Israel. Manasseh was caught, bound, and taken prisoner to Babylon. Interestingly enough, Chronicles further describes how Manasseh repented, was restored to his kingdom, and thereafter attempted to correct the wrongs he had caused.

The Man of God and an Unnamed Prophet that came to King Amaziah, circa 839–809 B.C.
2 Chronicles 25

Amaziah reigned twenty-nine years in Jerusalem. On one occasion when he was preparing to go to war, he invited the armies of the children of Ephraim to join him. The man of God came to him and told him he did not need those armies and that God would deliver him. Amaziah complained because he had already paid the Ephraimite armies, but the man of God said God could reward him much more than he had paid. Amaziah sent the Ephraimites home and, as prophesied by the man of God, defeated the armies of Seir.

But then Amaziah made a mistake. When he took the spoils of the Edomites, he took the gods of the Edomites with him and "set them up to be his gods, and bowed down himself before them, and burned incense unto them." God became angry at this and sent another unnamed prophet to Amaziah. Amaziah did not know him, therefore, it can be concluded that it was a different prophet. He asked Amaziah why he was worshiping gods that could not deliver the armies of the Edomites from Amaziah's forces. But this logic was of no avail. Amaziah would not heed the counsel of the second unnamed prophet and turned away from the Lord. The prophet then told Amaziah that because he would not heed the Lord's counsel and cease worshiping false gods, the God of Israel would destroy him.

In time, a conspiracy formed against Amaziah in Jerusalem. He fled to avoid his enemies, but he was finally caught in Lachish and killed.

The Unnamed Prophet, and a Man of the Sons of the Prophets that came to Ahab, circa 919–896 B.C.
1 Kings 20

This is one of several unique stories found in the annals of the Old Testament. It is intertwined with the story of Elijah, but neither of the prophets involved in the story is Elijah.

Ahab was warring with Benhadad, the king of Syria. In the midst of the conflict an unnamed prophet came to Ahab and declared that the Lord had delivered the host of Syria into his hands. Ahab immediately ordered his army into battle—while Benhadad drank himself into oblivion. The army of Israel defeated the Syrians and the prophet again came to Ahab and told him to prepare for a year because the Syrians would come up against him again at that time. Meanwhile, Benhadad acknowledged God, but only as the God of the mountains and not the valleys because Israel had only defeated him in the mountains. Again a "man of God" (assumed here to be the same unnamed prophet that prophesied to him earlier) came to Ahab and told him that because Benhadad said God was only the God of the mountains and not the valleys, Israel would completely defeat him. The battle commenced and Israel won, and those Syrians that were not killed fled for their lives. Benhadad's counselors counseled him to give up so that the lives of his people would be spared. He surrendered and Ahab spared their lives. Then the story really becomes unique.

A man, one of the sons of the prophets, commanded his neighbor to "smite" him. The neighbor refused and the man stated that because he had refused, a lion would slay him. And it did! The man then approached another individual and told him to "smite" (kill) him. This time the individual tried, but he only resulted in wounding him. The man (who is now called a prophet) departed, disguised himself, and waited for Ahab. Ahab arrived and the prophet told him the following story in parable form: during a battle a man was entrusted with a prisoner and was told to watch him so that he didn't escape. If he escaped, the man would forfeit his life or "pay a talent of silver" as a punishment (a condition that seems to have no bearing on the story). Eventually, however, the man got busy and did not notice when the prisoner escaped. Ahab judged the man's actions and said he should be punished in accordance with the requirements of his watch. The prophet then removed his disguise and Ahab discovered that he was a prophet—how, we are not told. The prophet then pronounced the judgment of the Lord: because Ahab had let Benhadad and those with him who had surrendered remain alive, Ahab's life would be taken instead of Benhadad's, and the people of Israel would fall instead of the people of Syria. It all came to pass. An unusual story to say the least.

Section IV
Divided Israel
The Southern Kingdom

The Southern Kingdom was also called the Kingdom of Judah. When Israel divided, the Northern Kingdom retained ten tribes and the Southern Kingdom was given only one tribe: Judah. The tribe of Benjamin was not included in either kingdom; however, geographically it was side by side with Judah and had always been associated with it. Shortly after the division, most of the tribe of Benjamin affiliated with Judah along with stray remnants of all the tribes that remained living in the cities of Judah at that time. Rehoboam, son of Solomon, was the first king of the Southern Kingdom.

Shemaiah

972 B.C.
1 Kings 12:22–24; 2 Chronicles 11:2–4; 12

The name Shemaiah means, *the Lord heareth*, or *heard by Jeho-vah*. Very little information is known about him. He was a prophet during the reign of Rehoboam, king of Judah, and he wrote a book chronicling the events of the reign of Rehoboam, one of the lost books of the Bible. But there are only two instances where his ministry to the king and the children of Judah is recorded.

Immediately after the division of Israel into the northern and southern kingdoms, Rehoboam decided he would go to war against Jeroboam in an attempt to bring the kingdom back together. He assembled one hundred and eighty thousand men from the tribes of Judah and Benjamin to fight against Jeroboam, but the "word of God" came to Shemaiah. He was told to inform Rehoboam that it was God's will that the kingdom be split and that they should not go up to fight against their "brethren," the children of Israel. It's obvious that Shemaiah was well-known to the king and was accepted as a prophet of the Lord, because immediately after the declaration of God's will by Shemaiah, Rehoboam dispersed the soldiers and all returned to their homes.

The only other time we hear of Shemaiah is when King Shishak of Egypt started a war against Jerusalem. The scripture states that Rehoboam and his people "forsook the law of the Lord," and be-

Prophets of the Old Testament

cause of this transgression, the Lord sent Shishak against them. He came with a huge army: twelve hundred chariots and sixty thousand horsemen, and they conquered many of the cities of Judah until they came to Jerusalem. Then came Shemaiah.

Shemaiah delivered the word of the Lord to Rehoboam and the princes of Judah saying, because they had forsaken the Lord, the Lord had delivered them into the hands of Shishak. Just as before, the princes of Judah listened to Shemaiah and humbled themselves before the Lord. The Lord saw their contriteness and accepted it. He told Shemaiah He would not destroy them and although His wrath would be poured out against the inhabitants of Jerusalem, He would "grant them some deliverance." Shishak sacked Jerusalem, including the house of the Lord and the king's palace, but he spared the people, and the wrath of the Lord was turned away from both Rehoboam and Judah.

Six Prophets and a Prophetess

Azariah, 939 B.C.
2 Chronicles 15:1–8

Azariah was a common name in Israel, especially among the priests. The name means *whom the Lord helps.* Azariah was the son of Obed and the first of four prophets who mysteriously appeared in the kingdom of Judah, delivered some prophecy or message from the Lord, and then disappeared as mysteriously as they appeared.

The scriptures introduce Azariah by stating that the Spirit of God came upon him and he went to meet with King Asa and all the people of Judah and Benjamin. He told them that the Lord would be with them if they were with the Lord, but if they forsook the Lord, He would forsake them (a message similar to that delivered by Shemaiah.) He recited some general history of Israel which indicated that when they believed in the Lord and lived His commandments, they were at peace. When they stopped believing, however, they were destroyed. Azariah also said that they had been a long time without God, a teaching priest, and the law. He encouraged them to be strong in their reliance upon the Lord.

Asa repented when he heard the words Azariah (and a prophecy Oded had made that was apparently rehearsed by Azariah).

He removed the false idols in Judah and restored the altar of the Lord. He called the people of Judah and Benjamin together (along with members of the other tribes that had joined them) and offered sacrifice to the Lord.

Although this is the only reference in scripture to the prophet Azariah, it is obvious that he had a great influence on the king and a profound effect upon the kingdom of Judah.

Hanani, 941 B.C.
2 Chronicles 16:1–10

Hanani, whose name means *gracious,* is the second prophet to briefly appear to Asa, king of Judah. Hanani was a seer. At the time of Hanani, Judah was at war with King Baasha of Israel. Baasha was building a fortress at Ramah and because Asa wanted to stop the construction he sent gold and silver to Benhadad, king of Syria and made a league with him to fight against Israel. Syria consequently joined Judah and helped defeat the armies of Israel.

Now Hanani appears. He came to King Asa and told him that his reliance on Syria (rather than on the Lord) was an error. He enumerated several historical examples where the Lord had given Asa victory over his enemies. He told Asa he had acted foolishly and because of his failure to rely on the Lord, he would have only wars throughout his reign (presumably against Syria). Asa became enraged and put Hanani in prison—and there his story ends. No other instance of his ministry is recorded, nor are there any records of his release from prison or his death.

Jahaziel, 896 B.C.
2 Chronicles 20:14–18

Jahaziel, whose name means *whom God watches over,* is the third prophet who appears to the kings of Judah in this sequence.

He only appears once in scripture to give a short prophecy amidst the congregation at the time of Jehoshaphat, the son and successor of King Asa. The scriptures recite a short genealogy to indicate that Jehaziel was of the tribe of Levi.

The countries of Ammon and Moab, neighbors of Judah, were preparing to engage Judah in war. Jehoshaphat prayed to the Lord for His assistance because there appeared to be no way to prevent the two nations from being victorious. Jahaziel stood up in the midst of the congregation and delivered his prophecy. He told Jehoshaphat and the people not to be afraid, but to go up to battle against Ammon and Moab. He even told them where to go for the battle: "up by the cliff of Ziz . . . at the end of the brook before the wilderness of Jeruel." He then indicated that the Lord would be with them and they would prevail. "Ye shall not need to fight in this battle: set yourselves, stand ye still, and see the salvation of the Lord with you."

The Spirit that motivated Jahaziel obviously fell upon Jehoshaphat and his people because they believed Jahaziel and fell down and worship the Lord. And the Lord blessed them and set "ambushments against the children of Ammon, Moab, and mount Seir, which were come against Judah; and they were smitten. For the children of Ammon and Moab stood up against the inhabitants of mount Seir, utterly to slay and destroy them: and when they had made an end of the inhabitants of Seir, every one helped to destroy another. And when Judah came toward the watch tower in the wilderness, they looked unto the multitude, and , behold, they were dead bodies fallen to the earth, and none escaped." All that was required of Judah was to gather the spoils, "both riches with the dead bodies, and precious jewels, which they stripped off for themselves, more than they could carry away"—for which they sang praises unto the Lord.

Eliezer, 895 B.C.
1 Kings 22:48; 2 Chronicles 20:35–37

The name of the prophet Eliezer means *God is his help.* He is only mentioned once in scripture. His father was Dodavah of Mareshah, and that is the only personal information we have about him. He is the fourth prophet in this chapter who briefly appears to the kings of Judah.

King Jehoshaphat of Judah had joined with King Ahaziah of Israel to build ships to go to Tarshish. Apparently the venture between the two kings involved the acquisition of gold. However, the scripture specifically notes that Ahaziah was very wicked.

The Lord obviously did not approve of this partnership because Eliezar prophesied against Jehoshaphat, saying "Because thou hast joined thyself with Ahaziah, the Lord hath broken they works." And the ships the kings were having constructed at Eziongeber were "broken," so that they were not able to go to Tarshish.

No detail is provided telling us *how* the ships were broken, and nothing else is known of Eliezer.

Zechariah, 807 B.C.
2 Chronicles 26:5

This Zechariah (not to be confused with the prophet who wrote the book of Zechariah) was a prophet and counselor to Uzziah, king of the Southern Kingdom. Uzziah was only sixteen years old when he began to reign in Jerusalem and he reigned for fifty-two years. He was a righteous king, according to all that his father, Amaziah, did. Uzziah's interaction with Zechariah occurred when he "sought God in the days of Zechariah." The scriptures further describe Zechariah as one "who had understanding in the visions of God." There is no other information about him. He is mentioned in only one verse.

Urijah, 608 B.C.
Jeremiah 26

This is an interesting prophet. Urijah, whose name means *light of Jehovah*, prophesied during the time of Jeremiah. His story appeared when Jeremiah had been condemned to die by the priests of Johoiakim, king of Judah. The condemned Jeremiah informed the assembly that they could do what they wanted with him, but if they killed him, they would bring innocent blood upon themselves. This seems to have pricked the hearts of the princes of Judah who then presented arguments against the priests, indicating that Jeremiah had done nothing to warrant death, but had spoken in the name of the Lord. They raised several examples of other prophets who had spoken ill against the land: Micah in the days of Hezekiah and then Urijah who was a contemporary of the times.

Urijah had prophesied against the land according "to all the words of Jeremiah." In other words, he was not only a contemporary of Jeremiah but agreed with him, and testified of the wickedness of the people and rulers. The king, as with Jeremiah, also sought Urijah's life. Urijah heard of the threat and fled to Egypt, but King Jehoiakim was relentless. He sent men to Egypt to find Urijah. They found him and brought him back to face Jehoiakim.

Jehoiakim executed Urijah with the sword (cut off his head), and cast his body in the "graves of the common people." He died a prophet-martyr before the destruction of Jerusalem by Nebuchadnezzar, king of Babylon. Nothing more is said of him.

Huldah the Prophetess, 623 B.C.
2 Kings 22:14–20; 2 Chronicles 34:22–28

The name Huldah means *weasel.* She appeared at the time of King Josiah of Judah—who began his reign when he was eight years old. Josiah was twenty-six when Hilkiah, his high priest, found a book of the Law while they were in the process of repairing the temple. The book was read before the king and he rent his clothes when he heard it (a common act of deep fear and concern in the Old Testament) because he immediately recognized that if the book were authentic, the people had not been living the commandments of the Lord and were therefore subject to the punishments recorded therein. Josiah wanted to authenticate the book and the information it contained, so he sent Hilkiah and others to inquire of the Lord concerning it. They went to Huldah the prophetess who dwelt in Jerusalem "in the college." (The reference to "college" probably indicates one of the schools of the prophets.) Her husband was the "keeper of the wardrobe."

Presumably, after hearing how the book had been found and then reading it herself, Huldah pronounced it as the word of the Lord. She prophesied that the Lord would bring evil upon Jerusalem and its inhabitants because they had not adhered to the commandments the book contained. Because of this, God's wrath would be against them.

Huldah continued and said because King Josiah was young and his heart "tender," and because he had humbled himself before the Lord, the Lord had heard him. God would honor Josiah because Josiah had honored God. But the Israelites had been (and continued to be) so wicked that God could not spare them—even for Josiah. He said he would bring evil upon Judah, "and upon the inhabitants thereof . . . Because they have forsaken me, and have burned incense unto other gods, that they provoke me to anger with all the works of their hands; therefore my wrath shall be poured out upon this place, and shall not be quenched." Fortunately, none of this would occur during Josiah's lifetime. Because of his righteousness, he would have peace. (But after he was laid to rest, the nation of Judah would suffer all that Huldah prophesied.)[96]

Hilkiah returned to Josiah and told him all that Huldah had said. When Josiah heard the report, he called the people together

---

[96] Josephus: Antiquities: 10.4.2, 3.

and made a covenant to live the commandments, to which all the people assented. To ensure that the people would keep the covenant, Josiah attempted to destroy the false places of worship and the pagan idols throughout the kingdom which also fulfilled the prophecy of the *man of God out of Judah* that said the false gods and altars that Jeroboam had built would be destroyed.[97]

There is no other information about Huldah in the scriptures.

[97] See page 5, "A Man of God out of Judah & The Old Prophet from Bethel."

Joel

800 B.C.
Book of Joel

The name Joel means *to whom Jehovah is God.* The actual date of Joel's ministry is uncertain. It may have been as early as 850 B.C., or after the return of the Israelites from captivity between 525–450 B.C. The book of Joel opens with the statement that the word of the Lord came to Joel, ". . . the son of Pethuel, . . ." and from there moves right into his prophecy.

Joel's prophecies are couched in the natural calamities of drought and the invasions of locusts that had befallen the people. He promised the people that if they repented, these adversities would be overcome and the blessings of the Lord would return. But his prophecies had a double reference that also applied to the future: to the time of Peter and the Apostles, to the day of the restoration of the gospel in the latter days, and to the Second Coming of the Lord in the fullness of time.

On the day of Pentecost, Peter quoted from Joel concerning the outpouring of the Spirit. "This is that which was spoken by the prophet Joel; And it shall come to pass in the last days, saith God, I will pour out my Spirit upon all flesh: and your sons and your daughters shall prophesy, and your young men shall see visions, and your old men shall dream dreams: And . . . my handmaidens . . . shall prophesy." In addition, Peter continued quoting from Joel, applying the prophecy to both his day and to the latter days. "And I will shew wonders in heaven above, and signs in the earth beneath; blood, and fire, and vapour of smoke: The sun shall be turned into darkness, and the moon into blood, before that great and notable day of the Lord come."[98]

Peter took this information from Joel 2:28–32, and Moroni presaged the restoration of the gospel in its fulness by quoting this scripture four times during his visits to Joseph Smith on the night of September 21 and the morning of September 22, 1823. Moroni declared that Joel's prophecy had not yet been fulfilled, but soon would be—all in anticipation of the revelations that would accompany the restoration and the signs that would occur before the Lord's Advent.

Joel concluded his book by citing the retribution the Lord would take against Egypt and Edom because of their violence against the children of Judah. Egypt would be "a desolation," and Edom would become "a desolate wilderness"—not only because of their violence, but because they had "shed innocent blood in their land." Then he ended on a note of hope, stating, "Judah shall dwell forever, and Jerusalem from generation to generation. For I will cleanse their blood that I have not cleansed: for the Lord dwelleth in Zion."

[98] Acts 2:16–21.

Isaiah

758–698 B.C.
Book of Isaiah

The name Isaiah means *salvation of Jahu* (a shortened form of Jehovah), or *the Lord is salvation.* Isaiah was the son of Amoz, and Amoz, according to Jewish tradition, was the brother of Amaziah, king of Judah.[99] Isaiah prophesied and ministered during the reign of four kings in Judah: Uzziah, Jotham, Ahaz, and Hezekiah. In addition, he was the chief political advisor to Hezekiah. The scriptures also tell us he was married and had two sons.

Isaiah's writings are quoted extensively in the New Testament, the Doctrine & Covenants, and in the Book of Mormon (the prophet Nephi declared that his soul delighted in the "words of Isaiah").[100] In the Doctrine & Covenants he is quoted more than any other prophet.

There is some controversy about the authorship of the book of Isaiah. Some critics feel that Isaiah wrote the first thirty-nine chapters of the book, but that a second Isaiah (or some other writer) wrote the last twenty-seven chapters. There are at least three arguments that discredit this contention. First, all of the New Testament quotes are attributed to Isaiah, regardless from which chapter in his book they were drawn. Second, the early Book of Mor-

---

[99] Smith's Bible Dictionary: Amoz.   [100] 2 Nephi 25:5.

mon prophets were familiar with the Old Testament texts of the Jews and the authors they attributed them to, and they said nothing of a second writer in Isaiah. Third, while working on the inspired version of the Bible, Joseph Smith left the book of Isaiah under Isaiah's authorship and did not refer to a second author.

Providing a general description (or categorizing the material within) any single chapter of Isaiah is difficult. For example, in the first chapter, which is generally described by most as the prologue to the rest of his book, there are multiple topics, discussed in various ways, using a range of descriptive analogies. The chapter is roughly divided into three categories: verses 1–15 which cover the topics of apostasy and the rebellion of the children of Israel; verses 16–25 which call the Israelites to repentance from the sins they have committed, and verses 26–31 which prophesy of the judgment that will come upon Israel and Israel's eventual restoration to a favored place with the Lord. The material contained in most of the subsequent chapters provides a quintessential example of the way the Lord reveals His secrets through His prophets.

Many of Isaiah's chapters can be generalized into such categories as historical, Second Coming, last days, the millennium, the gathering, the burden or prophecy of doom on a given country or people, and other miscellaneous topics. But upon detailed analysis, a reader soon discovers that although some or most of a chapter may deal with an identified topic, there are other layers of meaning within its verses—a double reference as it were, to other times and places.

When the word of the Lord was revealed to Isaiah, it not only jumped from topic to topic within chapters, but frequently jumped from one time period to another. This is what I mean by *double reference prophecy*. A given scripture can apply to two or more periods of time and to two or more groups of people. A good example of this is Isaiah 29:1–8. The scripture is speaking of Jerusalem (which may also represent all Israel) and what will eventually happen to the city and its people because of their wickedness. The prophecy and description could be describing the siege and conquest of Jerusalem by Nebuchadnezzar in 590–570 B.C., a hundred or so years after the death of Isaiah; however, it could also be describing the siege and conquest of Jerusalem by the Roman general Titus in A.D. 70, more than seven hundred years after the death of Isaiah. Or it could even be describing the great army that will besiege and eventually conquer Jerusalem just before the Second Coming of Christ, as depicted by Zechariah[101]—an event yet in the future that could occur more than three thousand years after the death of Isaiah. Or it could be describing all three events.

Isaiah primarily spoke to the Southern Kingdom (the Kingdom of Judah), but he also spoke of the great sins and the coming destruction of the Northern Kingdom (the Kingdom of Israel) which would occur within his lifetime. In addition to these two divisions, he also envisioned the dealings of the Lord with Israel as a whole, with the individual nations that surrounded the promised land, and occasionally with all people and all nations. And to further complicate his book, he spoke of these circumstances as if they were in the historical past, or during his lifetime, or at some point in the future. An example of this is found in Chapter 14. He begins that chapter with the gathering of Israel prior to the Second Coming and describes the peace and rest the people will have after the Lord comes. He also describes Lucifer and the reasons for his fall from greatness as "the son of the morning," and when he will be looked upon with wonder at the final judgment, and considered *small*. He then moves on to the description of the final destruction of all the wicked prior to the beginning of the millennium. All this in one chapter!

Isaiah begins his "burden" prophecies with Chapter 13. As used in those chapters, "burden" means doom, judgment, or destruction. He continues these prophecies through Chapter 23 (excluding Chapter 14) as succeeding nations and peoples are reviewed by the Lord and found wanting. Almost all of these chapters deal not only in *double reference*, to various people and periods

---

[101] Zechariah 12–14.

of time, but with numerous topics as well. They include the magnificent description of Egypt's relationship with Israel from the ancient past to the present and beyond. They also include Isaiah's requirement to go "naked" for three years as a sign to both Egypt and Ethiopia of their future captivity by Assyria.

Isaiah also spoke of events in his own time. He delivered the Lord's message of death to Hezekiah and when Hezekiah prayed with all his heart to live because he had been righteous, the Lord changed His mind and directed Isaiah back to Hezekiah to deliver a message of healing, indicating that he would extend Hezekiah's life for fifteen years. To confirm this blessing, Hezekiah was given a unique and specific sign: the sundial would reverse itself—it would move backwards ten degrees!

Although Isaiah provides little detail about his personal life, he succinctly describes the following important incidents:

1. His prophetic calling: "And I heard the voice of the Lord, saying, Whom shall I send, and who will go for us? Then said I, Here am I; send me. And he said, Go, and tell this people, Hear ye indeed, but understand not; and see ye indeed, but perceive not . . . Then said I, Lord, how long? And he answered, Until the cities be wasted without inhabitant, and the houses without man, and the land be utterly desolate."

2. His vision of the Lord: "I saw . . . the Lord sitting upon a throne, high and lifted up, and his train filled the temple. Above it stood the seraphims."

3. The symbolic purging of his sins when a hot coal is touched to his lips during the vision recorded in Chapter 6: "Then flew one of the seraphims unto me, having a live coal in his hand, which he had taken with the tongs from off the altar: And he laid it upon my mouth, and said, Lo, this hath touched thy lips; and thine iniquity is taken away, and thy sin purged."

Isaiah wrote in what is called *poetic prophecy*, an awe-inspiring writing style unsurpassed by any other prophet. He prophesied of the birth of Jesus Christ and described His life, including details about His treatment by the chosen people, His sorrows, crucifixion, and His atonement: "[T]o whom is the arm of the Lord revealed? For he shall grow up before him as a tender plant, and as a root out of a dry ground: he hath no form nor comeliness; and when we shall see him, there is no beauty that we should desire him. He is despised and rejected of men; a man of sorrows, and acquainted with grief." All this and more is found in Chapter 53, a rare chapter with a singular topic. Isaiah wrote on numerous occasions about the Second Coming of Christ and described in great detail the destruction that will precede the Lord's Advent and the millennial peace that will follow it.

Isaiah encouraged all people to "Arise, shine;" he explained, "for thy light is come, and the glory of the Lord is risen upon thee." This scripture has been loosely interpreted to mean, *Get thee up and be illuminated, or sit thee down and be eliminated.*" In other words, get off the fence and do something, reminiscent of what John records in Revelation when the Lord expressed to the Laodiceans: "I would thou wert cold or hot. So then because thou art lukewarm, and neither cold nor hot, I will spue thee out of my mouth."[102] Isaiah then delivered this moving description of living conditions during the Lord's millennial reign.

"Violence shall no more be heard in thy land, wasting nor destruction within thy borders; but thou shall call thy walls Salvation, and thy gates Praise. The sun shall be no more thy light by day; neither for brightness shall the moon give light unto thee: but the Lord shall be unto thee an everlasting light, and thy God thy glory. Thy sun shall no more go down; neither shall thy moon withdraw itself: for the Lord shall be thine everlasting light, and the days of thy mourning shall be ended. Thy people also shall be all righteous: they shall inherit the land for ever . . . ."

The scriptures are silent concerning Isaiah's death, but Rabbinical tradition says he was cut asunder while in the trunk of a

[102] Revelation 3:15, 16.

carob tree during the reign of Manasseh (perhaps a procedure that Paul was familiar with since he referred to prophets being "sawn asunder" in his Epistle to the Hebrews).[103] But the important thing to remember is that Isaiah was a great prophet and the preferred advisor to kings for almost sixty years. And considering the variety of topics he covered, it's no wonder he's the most quoted prophet in the Old Testament.

---

[103] Hebrews 11:37.

Micah

740–697 B.C.
Book of Micah

Micah's name means *who is like Jehovah*. He declares himself to be a Morasthite, or of the city of Moresheth in the plain country of Judea. His ministry took place during the reign of three kings of Judah: Jotham, Ahaz, and Hezekiah. He was a contemporary of Hosea and Amos during their ministry to the Northern Kingdom, and of Isaiah in the Southern Kingdom. Nothing else is known of his personal life.

The first part of Micah's book deals with the impending and immediate judgment of Israel by the Lord. In keeping with their history, Israel is again in sin. Micah enumerates those sins in Chapter 3. They include idolatry, neglect of the poor by the rich, and the seeking of riches above other things. Chapter 4 begins with two unique verses that contain the same information found in the introductory verses to Isaiah Chapter 2. ". . . In the last days it shall come to pass, that the mountain of the house of the Lord shall be established in the top of the mountains, and it shall be exalted above the hills; and people shall flow unto it. And many nations shall come, and say, Come, and let us go up to the mountain of the Lord, and to the house of the God of Jacob; and he will teach us of his ways, and we will walk in his paths: for the law shall go forth [out] of Zion, and the word of the Lord from Jerusalem." Micah then continues with a grand description of the millennium.

Chapter 5 contains the only Messianic prophecy identifying Bethlehem as the birthplace of the Savior. "But thou, Bethlehem Ephratah, though thou be little among the thousands of Judah, yet out of thee shall he come forth unto me that [who] is to be ruler in Israel; whose goings forth have been from of old, from everlasting." When the wise men from the east asked Herod where the king of the Jews would be born, Herod had his priests review the scriptures and after they found the Micah prophecy, he directed the wise men to Bethlehem.[104] This chapter also contains the prophecies of the gathering and the restoration of Jacob (or Israel) as well as additional millennial descriptions and information on the millennial reign of Jesus.

In Chapter 6, Micah declares that the "Lord hath a controversy with his people." He questions what is to be done to overcome the controversy and answers with the Lord's three-pronged requirement that His people "do justly . . . love mercy . . . and . . . walk humbly with thy God."

Although Micah deals with the usual problems of a disobedient Israel, the judgments of the Lord as a result of that disobedience, and the resulting punishment Israel will receive, he also relies heavily on the ultimate mercy of the Lord to eventually gather His children and pardon them, promising the reader that God will not retain "his anger for ever."

---

[104] Matthew 2:1–6.

Nahum

circa 663–612 B.C.

Book of Nahum

The only information we have about Nahum, whose name means *comfort, consoler,* or *consolation*, comes from his book. He states that he is an Elkoshite. Some have placed that community in Galilee, others say it's in Assyria.[105] There is no specific evidence of the date of his book, but since it deals with the "burden" or doom of Nineveh and the destruction of the Assyrian Empire, it had to have been written prior to 625 B.C. when Nineveh was destroyed by the Medes and the Chaldeans.

Although Jonah had prophesied of the destruction of Nineveh some one hundred and fifty years earlier, because of the people's repentance at that time the city was spared. (A prophecy of the destruction of Nineveh was also given by the prophet Zephaniah.)[106]

At Nahum's time, the city was at the height of its glory and the center of commerce in the then known world. It was an extremely large city, estimated to be three miles wide and eight miles long. The Tigris River formed its western and southern boundaries and a wall protected the eastern and northern boundaries. Suburbs extended as far as fourteen miles north and twenty miles south. When Jonah visited the city, it took three days to walk across it

---

[105] Smith's Bible Dictionary: Nahum.   [106] Zephaniah 2:13–15.

from border to border.[107]   The Assyrians considered it (and perhaps their entire empire) impregnable.   Nahum refers to it as the
"bloody city . . . full of lies and robbery." He prophesied its complete destruction and concluded that even though the Lord used
the Assyrians to punish and destroy the Northern Kingdom, because of their extreme cruelty and wickedness they (and Nineveh)
would now be destroyed, never to rise again.

Most scholars count Nahum as one of the great poets of his
time. They consider his language to be classical, the sentences
balanced and sprinkled with alliteration and rare idioms, and they
ranked him among the most gifted writers of the Old Testament.[108]

Nothing is known of his death.

---

[107] Jonah 3:3.   [108] Catholic Encyclopedia: Nahum.

Jeremiah

626–586 B.C.
Book of Jeremiah, Lamentations

Jeremiah, whose name means *whom Jehovah has appointed,* was probably born during the reign of King Amon of Judah. He was the son of Hilkiah who was one "of the priests that were in Anathoth." He was called as a young man to the prophetic office and began his service as a prophet during the thirteenth year of the reign of Josiah. He continued his work after the death of Josiah through the next four kings of Judah (Jehoahaz, Jehoiakim, Jehoichin, and Zedekiah) and through the downfall of Jerusalem, a period of more than forty years. He was a contemporary of Ezekiel, Daniel, and Zephaniah, although there is no evidence that any of them knew each other. His ministry was one of turmoil, both for himself and for the people.

When the Lord called to Jeremiah He told him that he had been called to be a prophet before he was born. Jeremiah responded, as had other prophets before him, by stating, "Aw, Lord God! behold, I cannot speak: for I am a child." The Lord refuted that and told him that he would go wherever the Lord sent him. Then he comforted Jeremiah by saying, "Be not afraid . . . for I am with thee to deliver thee." The Lord then touched Jeremiah's mouth with His finger, symbolically telling Jeremiah that He had "put [His] words in [his] mouth." His call would not be easy nor his words encouraging; but the Lord had set Jeremiah "over the nations and over the kingdoms, to root out, and to pull down, and to destroy, and to throw down, to build, and to plant."

Jeremiah's calls to repentance were couched in strong terms. He condemned false worship, false alliances, and false prophets. He enumerated the sins of kings, nations, people, and priests. He delivered the condemnation of the Lord upon all their evil acts and told them they would be punished by defeat in battle, by destruction, and by captivity. He offered them salvation time and time again if they would return and worship the true God, but the people and the kings who succeeded Josiah would not. He fearlessly delivered the messages of an angry God because the people had deserted Him and were worshiping false gods. "Seest thou not what they do?" the Lord asked Jeremiah. But Jeremiah could see what they were doing. They were kindling sacrificial fires in the streets of Jerusalem. The women were preparing cakes to offer to the "queen of heaven." The Lord was so angry with Judah's faithlessness and false worship that He told Jeremiah He would cast her people out, just as He had her brethren of the tribe of Ephraim. Then the Lord issued what is perhaps His most condemnatory order recorded in the Old Testament: "Therefore pray not thou for this people, neither lift up cry nor prayer for them, neither make intercession to me: *for I will not hear thee.*" (Emphasis added.)

Because of his determination to deliver both the Lord's offer of repentance and His angry condemnations, Jeremiah had to face continuous persecution. The people believed—nay, from their perspective they *knew* they were not sinning—and false prophets kept telling them all was well. As a result, Jeremiah was continually opposed and insulted by the priests and religious leaders of his day. He was railed upon by mobs that tormented him. His own townspeople of Anathoth sought to kill him and even his brethren, members of his own father's family, dealt "treacherously" with him that they might deliver him to the multitude. Countless times he was insulted and chastised, and many sought to destroy him— from the common people, to the king, to the armies of Judah. He was perhaps the most tormented and persecuted prophet in the Old Testament.

Jeremiah continually buttressed the delivery of his messages with introductions such as "the word of the Lord came to me". . . "saith the Lord" . . . and "for thus saith the Lord," all of which were used more than a hundred times in his book in order to emphasize to the people that God knew what they were doing, regardless of what they thought or what others told them. So open was the Lord through Jeremiah that it left them no excuse; for "the least of them even unto the greatest of them" was "given to covetousness; and from the prophet even unto the priest," they all dealt falsely with the Lord and with one another.

King Josiah initially sought to restore the people to the true worship of God, but they would not. And upon Josiah's death, successive rulers were only characterized as being evil. With some indication that the schools of the prophets were still operating, the Lord said that "the prophets prophesy falsely, and the priests bear rule by their means; and my people love to have it so."

Jeremiah prophesied that Babylon would soon conquer Judah and carry the people off into captivity. To emphasize the prophecy, the Lord had Jeremiah wear a linen girdle and then hide it in "a hole of the rock." After some days the Lord commanded Jeremiah to retrieve the girdle. He did so and found that it was "marred," and "profitable for nothing." So also "will I mar the pride of Judah," the Lord said, and "it shall be wholly carried away captive." The Lord finally expressed his utter disgust with Judah when he said: "I am weary with repenting."

The Lord commanded Jeremiah to neither marry nor have children because those that did would die "grievous deaths." Then the Lord commanded Jeremiah to provide the children of Judah with another "show and tell." He sent Jeremiah to a potter's house and had him watch the potter. But the vessel worked on became marred in the potter's hand and the Lord likened this to the house of Israel since Israel was in His hand to do with as he pleased. The people had become so wicked that they offered their sons and daughters to Baal as burnt offerings, undoubtedly motivating Jeremiah to utter one of his most destructive prophecies. He told the Israelites that their plight during the imminent siege of Jerusalem would become so great it would "cause them to eat the flesh of their sons and the flesh of their daughters." And then they would be conquered and live in captivity for seventy years.

Jeremiah was constantly using himself as an example of what would happen to the people because of their sin and their refusal to repent. He placed a wooden yoke upon his neck to show them the difficulty they would have in bondage. The false prophet Hananiah came before the people, took the yoke from Jeremiah's neck, broke it, and prophesied falsely that the threat of Babylon would be broken as was the yoke. The Lord had Jeremiah inform them that because Hananiah had spoke falsely and the people believed him, He would now place yokes of iron upon them, compounding the difficulty they would have during their bondage to Babylon. Then Jeremiah spoke to the false prophet Hananiah: "The Lord hath not sent thee;" he began, "but thou makest this people to trust in a lie." As a result of his teachings and the people's rebellion against the Lord, Jeremiah prophesied that Hananiah would die within the year—and he did.

So harsh were the words of Jeremiah that finally the princes at the time of Zedekiah had had enough. They "smote" him and put him in prison. But the siege by the armies of Babylon was so intense that the king sent to him "secretly" and asked if there was any word from the Lord—apparently expecting some type of miraculous deliverance. Jeremiah responded by again prophesying that Jerusalem would soon be conquered by the armies of Babylon. The princes and the people once more turned their anger toward him and threw him into a dungeon where "Jeremiah [sank] in the mire." Still the king persisted in requesting instructions from Jeremiah, so he gave him his final advice. He told him to surrender himself and all his family to the king of Babylon and they would survive and be well. But Zedekiah would not heed Jeremiah's words and attempted to escape. He was soon captured and experienced the horror of seeing his own sons mercilessly killed before the Babylonians put his eyes out. The cruel death of his sons was the last thing he saw.

Jeremiah survived the siege and saw firsthand the destruction of Jerusalem and the Lord's temple. He was then taken into captivity by the Babylonians, but Nebuchadnezzar treated him well. He told him he could go with the captives, stay in Jerusalem, or go anywhere he pleased. Jeremiah decided to stay in Jerusalem. Jeremiah told the surviving inhabitants (after the Babylonians had carried off the captives they wanted) that they should remain in the promised land; that if they did, all would be well with them. But if they disregarded his advice and went to Egypt, as was their expressed desire, they would again be captives because Egypt would fall as well. Again the people would not heed his words. They went to Egypt and Jeremiah went with them, but eventually Egypt fell.

It is presumed that the book of Jeremiah grew out of the roll or copy that Baruch, his servant, made. The first one was cut to pieces and burned by Jehudi who read portions of it to King Jehoiakim, but another was created. In it Jeremiah not only speaks of the destruction and captivity of the Southern Kingdom, but in Chapters 46–51 he prophesies the destruction of ten foreign nations. After these chapters, his succinct and astounding prophecies foretell the fall of Babylon, Judah's conqueror. He was labeled a prophet of doom by his contemporaries, yet he prophesied that God would restore the Jews to Jerusalem after the captivity in Babylon, and that the Lord would eventually gather all Israel, including all twelve tribes.

Because Lehi and his people left Jerusalem around 600 B.C. (during the time of Jeremiah) the Book of Mormon notes that some of the writings of Jeremiah were on the brass plates that were

---

[109] 1 Nephi 5:10–13.

retrieved from Laban.[109] Jeremiah is mentioned twice more within the Book of Mormon record.[110]

In addition to the book of Jeremiah, the book of Lamentations is also attributed to the writings of Jeremiah. It is a book of poetry, written by one who saw the sorrow it portrays. It laments the terrible destruction of a nation and its people, poetically expressing the personal depth of Jeremiah's sorrow. He lived through the destruction he prophesied—and neither the people nor the leadership did anything to prevent it.

As for Jeremiah's death, nothing is known. Tradition states that he was stoned by the very people he sought to save. And from the recorded persecutions he suffered and the tremendous animosity his words generated, it is a believable conclusion to his story.

[110] 1 Nephi 7:14; Helaman 8:20.

Zephaniah

642–611 B.C.
Book of Zephaniah

The name Zephaniah means *hidden by Jehovah,* or *the Lord hides.* He begins his book in the traditional manner by listing the names of four generations of his ancestors, but no other personal information is recorded.

Zephaniah prophesied during the reign of Josiah, king of Judah. He was a contemporary of Jeremiah, although there is no evidence that they knew each other. He speaks and prophesies concerning the imminent destruction of Jerusalem and the kingdom of Judah. But the essence of these prophecies contain a double reference to the events that will occur to both Jerusalem and to other nations before the Second Coming of the Lord. Consequently, he describes the near destruction of Jerusalem with such introductory terms as: "the great day of the Lord is near," and "in the day of the Lord's wrath."

Like Jeremiah, Zephaniah's, prophecy was not pleasant. He described the coming destruction of Jerusalem (at his time and in the future) as a "day of trouble and distress, a day of wasteness and desolation, a day of darkness and gloominess, a day of clouds and thick darkness," concluding that "the whole land shall be devoured by the fire of [the Lord's] jealousy."

He prophesied against the nations surrounding Israel and told of their eventual punishment and destruction (at the present and in the future) because they had "magnified themselves against the people of the Lord of hosts." The Lord indicated He would gather them and pour out His indignation upon them, even all His "fierce anger." Then Zephaniah gives a most interesting prophecy. After the destruction of the wicked, the Lord states He will restore a "pure language" to the people—perhaps in anticipation of the return of that language spoken in the Garden of Eden.

Zephaniah concludes his short work by turning to the time of the Second Coming. By that time, all who had done evil would be gone and those who remained would trust in the Lord. There would be no iniquity in them. They would not lie to one another, nor would a "deceitful tongue be found in their mouth." A totally honest people! He then speaks of the two world capitals—Jerusalem and Zion—stating that the Lord would be in their midst and His glory, and the glory of His people, would be known throughout the world.

Habakkuk

circa 600 B.C.
Book of Habakkuk

Habakkuk's book contains no personal information and he is not referenced anywhere else in the scriptures. Not even an interpretation of his name is provided. But because of the way his book is written, it's very interesting. The first two chapters of his three-chapter book are written as if he's speaking with God and God is answering: a question and answer dialogue.

The first question is in Chapter 1, verses 1–4. Habakkuk is concerned about a situation that has provided food for thought to philosophers over the centuries. "Why do the wicked prosper when they seem only to do wickedly?" and, "when will they be punished?" He is speaking of course, of the chosen people in the kingdom of Judah. The Lord answers him in verses 5–11 by stating that the wicked in Judah will be punished by the Chaldeans (the Babylonian empire), for they will conquer them and occupy the land. The Lord's answer raises another question. In Chapter 1, verses 12–17, Habakkuk appears to be saying, "Okay, but why the Chaldeans, because they are more wicked than the chosen people?" The Lord's reply comes in Chapter 2, verses 1–5, wherein He explains that Israel will be punished because of its wickedness. He goes on to say that He will also punish the Chaldeans because of their wickedness. Then Habakkuk records five "woes" that the Lord proclaims against the wicked. Each *woe* is a warning to them that describes the punishment that the Lord will mete out against them for their sins. The third and final chapter of Habakkuk is a prayer or poem intended to be sung. It is recorded by Habakkuk to praise and memorialize the Lord once Habakkuk is satisfied with their conversation.

Obadiah

588–583 B.C.
Book of Obadiah

The name Obadiah means *servant of the Lord.* Nothing is known of him other than that which can be gleaned from the short book that bears his name. The date of his ministry is derived from his reference in verse 11 to the captivity of Jerusalem, which is generally interpreted as the Nebuchadnezzar captivity.

The book of Obadiah is a scathing denunciation of the people of Edom (descendants of Abraham through Esau). Apparently the Edomites had displayed hostility toward Judah just before and during the time of her war with Babylon. That brought the displeasure of the Lord upon Edom. Obadiah describes the actions of the Edomites as if Edom were one of the besiegers. After Jerusalem was captured, Edom rejoiced. As a result, Obadiah prophesied that Edom would be cut off and slaughtered when the destruction of the heathen came upon them.

Obadiah also prophesied that eventually the house of Jacob (referring to Judah), and the house of Joseph would return to their possessions (the land of promise). And then "Esau," (the Edomites) would be as "stubble." The Lord appears to be defining the eventual destruction of those descendants of Abraham who are not under the Abrahamic Covenant and redefining the boundaries of the land of promise.[111]

[111] Obadiah 1:17–20.

Section V
The Babylonian Captivity

The Babylonian Captivity occurred when Nebuchadnezzar completed his conquest of the Southern Kingdom in approximately 570 B.C. His assault began in 596 B.C. and the captivity of the Jews lasted for approximately seventy years before they were again allowed to return to Jerusalem and the promised land.

Two prophets of record were functioning during this period: Daniel and Ezekiel. The prophets Ezra, Nehemiah, Haggai, and Zechariah were undoubtedly born during the captivity, but they are dealt with in Section VI, "Return from Captivity," because that's when their ministries occurred.

Daniel

604–534 B.C.
Book of Daniel

D aniel means *judgment of God,* or *a judge (is) God.* He is only
one of two prophets in the Old Testament who interpreted
dreams for others. (The other was Joseph of Egypt.) He is carried
off to Babylon in the third year of the reign of King Jehoiakim, the
reigning monarch in Judah when Nebuchadnezzar first conquered
Jerusalem. According to Nebuchadnezzaar's requirements for the
first captives taken after he conquered Jerusalem (as noted in Daniel
1:3), Daniel is assumed to be of royal descent or a descendant of
one of the princes of Judah. The captives that were taken to Babylon
were required to have no blemish, to be well-favored, to be skillful
in wisdom, cunning in knowledge, and to have an understanding
of the science of the day. There is no record of Daniel's personal
history prior to the captivity.

The first six chapters of the Book of Daniel contain a narrative
history of Daniel and his three friends, Hananiah, Mishael, and
Azariah while they are in captivity. All four of the captives have
their names changed by the Babylonians: Daniel to "Belteshazzar,"
which we do not remember him by; Hananiah to "Shadrach,"
Mishael to "Meshach," and Azariah to "Abednego"—names by
which these three are remembered. They, along with the other
unidentified captives, were to be taught the knowledge and language of the Chaldeans. They were set aside for such instruction

for a period of three years and prescribed a "diet" during that time by the king. But because Daniel would not "defile" himself by eating the king's meat nor drinking his wine, he requested a simpler diet of "pulse" (which usually meant beans, peas, and seeds of any kind that grew in pods)[112] and water to drink. The prince of the eunuchs was reluctant at first to deviate from the king's recommended diet but after a ten-day trial period, he agreed to the change. As time passed, the scripture notes: "As for these four children, God gave them knowledge and skill in all learning and wisdom: and Daniel had understanding in all visions and dreams." The king consulted with them and considered them "ten" times better than any other magician or astrologer in his realm. Then Nebuchadnezzar had his famous dream—that he could not remember! The circumstances are as follows:

Nebuchadnezzar awoke after having a distressing dream and "his spirit was troubled" to know what the dream meant, but he couldn't remember it. He called his magicians and astrologers together and asked them to tell him what his dream was and then to interpret it. They were astonished at this request and couldn't do it. They complained that no one could do it. Nebuchadnezzar became angry and sent out a decree ordering all of them slain. Since Daniel and his fellows were also considered magicians and astrologers, they fell under the king's decree. But Daniel had not heard about the king's problem, so when he was told that his life was in jeopardy, he went to Arioch, the captain of Nebuchadnezzar's guard, to find out why the decree had been issued. Arioch told him about the king's dream and the inability of his wise men to recall it. Daniel went to Nebuchadnezzar and told him that given a little time, he could tell him what his dream was and what it meant. The king granted him some time and Daniel returned to his house. That night the Lord revealed the secret of Nebuchadnezzar's dream to Daniel in a vision. The next day he went back to Arioch and said, "Destroy not the wise men of Babylon: [but]

---

[112] Smith's Bible Dictionary: Pulse.

bring me in before the king, and I will shew unto [him] the interpretation" of his dream.

Daniel told Nebuchadnezzar that in his dream he had seen a man-image. The man-image was composed of gold, silver, brass, iron, and clay. The various body parts of the man-image represented different kingdoms of the earth, beginning with the head of gold (Babylon) and extending into the future through the other metals to the toes of iron and clay. At the end of the dream, Daniel told the king that he had seen a stone which struck the man-image and broke it into pieces and that the stone's influence eventually filled the entire earth.

The stone in Nebuchadnezzar's dream represented the kingdom of God, which would fill the earth after the ten kingdoms came into existence. The kingdom of God would eventually supersede or infiltrate all national boundaries and grow until it eventually consumed all the kingdoms of the world.

When Nebuchadnezzar heard Daniel's interpretation, he "fell upon his face, and worshiped Daniel, and commanded that they should offer an oblation and sweet odours unto him." He made Daniel chief of all the wise men of Babylon and at Daniel's request, Shadrach, Meshach, and Abednego were appointed over the affairs of the province of Babylon.

The balance of the first six chapters of Daniel's book reveal an intrigue that was intended to entrap Daniel and his companions. Nebuchadnezzar had built a great golden image and commanded all his people to bow down and worship it whenever they heard the sound of "the cornet, flute, harp, sackbut, psaltery," or any kind of music. Those who would not bow down were to be thrown into a fiery furnace. Knowing that the golden image was a false deity, Shadrach, Meshach, and Abednego would not bow down and worship it. Consequently, they were accused by certain Chaldeans (who were the instigators in the creation of the image in the first place) of not complying with the king's commandment.

Shadrach, Meshach, and Abednego were then brought before the king and undoubtedly explained that they believed in the true God and could not worship Nebuchadnezzar's golden image. The king angrily threatened them with the fiery furnace and asked, "[W]ho *is* that God that shall deliver you out of my hands?" The three men replied, "O Nebuchadnezzar, we are not careful to answer thee in this matter. If it be so, our God whom we serve is able to deliver us from the burning fiery furnace . . . he will deliver us out of thine hand . . . But if not, be it known unto thee, O king, that we will not serve thy gods, nor worship the golden image which thou has set up."

Nebuchadnezzar became furious. He condemned Shadrach, Meshach, and Abednego to the fiery furnace and commanded that the furnace be heated to seven times its normal temperature. Then "he commanded the most mighty men . . . in his army to bind Shadrach, Meshach, and Abednego and to cast them into the burning fiery furnace." They were bound in "their coats, their hosen, and their hats, and their other garments, and were cast into the midst . . . of the burning fiery furnace." The furnace was so hot that the "flame of the fire slew those men that took up Shadrach, Meshach, and Abednego" as they threw them into the furnace.

When Nebuchadnezzar looked into the furnace, he was astonished. "Did we not cast three men bound into the midst of the fire?" he asked. His counselors affirmed that three men had been thrown into the flames. Then the king said, "Lo, I see four men loose, walking in the midst of the fire, and they have no hurt; and the form of the fourth is like the Son of God." We're not told how he knew it was the Son of God.

Nebuchadnezzar called out to Shadrach, Meshach, and Abednego, calling them "servants of the most high God," and told them to come forth out of the furnace. "And the princes, governors, and captains, and king's councillors, being gathered together, saw these men, upon whose bodies the fire had no power, nor was an hair of their head singed, neither were their coats changed, nor the smell of fire had passed on them." As a result of this miraculous occurrence, Nebuchadnezzar made a decree that any people or nation that spoke against the God of Shadrach, Meshach, and Abednego would be cut in pieces and their homes made into a "dunghill." He then "promoted Shadrach, Meshach, Abednego, in the province of Babylon."

Daniel interpreted many other dreams for Nebuchadnezzar. In one he disclosed a conspiracy that would succeed in dethroning Nebuchadnezzar. But he assured the king that eventually he would be reinstated to his kingdom—and all occurred as Daniel foretold.

The last of Daniel's interpretations occurred as a result of some handwriting on a wall. King Belshazzar, Nebuchadnezzar's son and successor, prepared a great feast and used the vessels his father had taken from the temple in Jerusalem as drinking cups. That's when the writing appeared on the wall. There came forth "fingers of a man's hand, and wrote over against the candlestick upon the plaister of the wall of the king's palace: and the king saw the part of the hand that wrote." The king was so frightened that "his knees smote one against another." Daniel was immediately called in to interpret the writing. He told Belshazzar that the words on the wall indicated that the days of Belshazzar's kingdom were numbered and would soon come to an end because the king had been "weighed in the balance" and was found wanting. The words continued and said, "Thy kingdom is divided, and given to the Medes and Persians." The prophecy came true. "In the night was Belshazzar the king of the Chaldeans slain," and "Darius the Median took the kingdom" and ruled in his stead.

The last story of Daniel's personal life involves the lion's den and another intriguing conspiracy. The "presidents and princes [of Babylon] sought to find occasion against Daniel concerning the kingdom," but they were thwarted in their attempts to dislodge him because except for his religious beliefs, they could find no "error or fault" in him. So the conspirators went before King Darius and convinced him to establish a royal decree that said: "[W]hosoever shall ask a petition of any God or man for thirty days, save of thee, O king . . . shall be cast into the den of lions." For some reason Darius agreed to sign this document and it went into effect.

When Daniel knew that the document had been signed, he went to his house, positioned himself in front of a window that was open toward Jerusalem, and kneeled upon his knees to pray. He prayed three times a day, giving thanks "before his God, as he did aforetime." Naturally, the conspirators were watching him and reported his activities to King Darius. They demanded that Darius comply with his decree and cast Daniel into the lion's den for his disobedience.

When the king heard their demands he was "sore displeased with himself" because he loved Daniel, and he "set his heart" to try to deliver Daniel from the terrible fate that awaited him. But it was to no avail. The next day when Daniel was placed in the lion's den, the king told him, "Thy God whom thou servest continually, he will deliver thee." A stone was placed on the mouth of the den and the king sealed it with his own signet, "and with the signet of his lords," so that nothing else could happen to Daniel during the night. The king then passed the night fasting for Daniel's survival, and you're probably familiar with the rest of the story. Daniel came out of the lion's den without a scratch.

The king then turned the tables on those who had conspired against Daniel. They and their families were tossed into the lion's den and suffered the fate they had intended for Daniel.

The balance of Daniel's book (Chapters 7–12) describes the visions he received. They are recorded in first person narrative, presumably by Daniel himself. The visions he received were those that had been (or would be) seen by other prophets in the Bible, and should be read in conjunction with Isaiah 24–27, Zechariah 9–14, and Revelation 7–22. They are apocalyptic in nature and concern events reserved for the future—including the period of time just prior to and during the Second Coming of Jesus Christ.

We are not told whether Daniel ever returned to Jerusalem. However, his life of unwavering obedience to the Lord and the

Lord's commandments is acknowledged as factual by other prophets. Ezekiel for instance acknowledged him as a pattern of wisdom who would deliver his own soul by his "righteousness."[113]

The words of other prophets also authenticate various elements of Daniel's book—such as miracles, prophecy, and the existence of angels. Paul writes about miracles that occurred in his time (and even notes Daniel's encounter with the lions);[114] The Lord reiterates Daniel's prophecy concerning the "abomination of desolation" as He foretells of the destruction of Jerusalem and the great devastation that will occur prior to the Second Coming;[115] and the existence of angels and their interaction with mankind is confirmed in the record of Luke.[116] From latter day revelation, we learn that when Daniel saw "One like unto a Son of Man," he was seeing Jesus Christ, and the individual he saw that the scriptures called the "Ancient of Days" was Adam (who is also know as "Michael").[117]

It's unfortunate that the scriptures contain nothing more about Daniel—neither the balance of his life nor the time or place of his death. But what we have gives us the privilege of learning about one of the Lord's most unique and powerful prophets, and provides a worthy example of unwavering faith for mankind to follow.

[113] Ezekiel 14:14, 20; 28:3.
[114] Hebrews 11:33.
[115] Matthew 24:15.
[116] Luke 1:19, 26.
[117] Doctrine & Covenants 116; 128:21.

Ezekiel

595–573 B.C.
Book of Ezekiel

The name Ezekiel means *the strength of God,* or *God will strengthen.* God used the phrase, "Son of man," when addressing Ezekiel on many occasions throughout his book. Ezekiel was the son of Buzi and a functioning priest when he was taken captive by the Babylonians at the time of King Jehoiachin of Judah—eleven years before the final fall of Jerusalem and complete captivity by Nebuchadnezzar. He lived in the area of Chebar, a river in Babylonia.

Ezekiel was the prophet of the captivity. He was a contemporary of Daniel and Jeremiah, although if they knew of each other or communicated, we're not told about it. Like Daniel of the Old Testament and John the Revelator in the New Testament, he was a visionary prophet. He was respected and consulted throughout the captivity by those who were captive with him, especially after his prophecies concerning the destruction of Jerusalem and the temple came true.

Chapter 1 of Ezekiel opens with Ezekiel's vision of four living creatures. Each creature had a face, four wings, and hands under its wings. Their feet were straight like a calf's foot and "sparkled" like burnished brass. Their faces were those of a man, a lion, an ox, and an eagle. (John the Revelator saw a similar vision in Revelation.)[118] In addition to their feet, the beasts had wheels, and each had "a wheel in the middle of a wheel." They also had rings, and the rings were full of eyes. Although Joseph Smith provided an interpretation of John's vision of the four beasts which sheds some light on the meaning of what Ezekiel saw (i.e., the beasts are full of knowledge and power and are figurative expressions to describe heaven, the paradise of God, the happiness of men and beasts, etc.),[118] how Ezekiel describes what he saw leaves almost everything to the imagination. (It is interesting to note that Ezekiel sees the same vision—or parts of it—several times throughout his book.)

During this vision (or in connection with it) Ezekiel has a vision of God. It begins as he describes the noise of the wings of the creatures he is seeing. He states that the noise is like the noise of "great waters, as the voice of the Almighty." The voice comes from the firmament above, which he envisions as "the likeness of a throne" and upon which is the "likeness as the appearance of a man." He describes the glory of this vision as being like fire, of the color of amber, and as the rainbow with brightness all around. And when he sees this glory, he falls "on his face" and heard a voice speak to him.

God then addresses Ezekiel as the "Son of man" and calls him to be a prophet, declaring that he is sending him "to the children of Israel." Next the Lord describes the children of Israel: they are "a rebellious nation . . . impudent, and stiff hearted." But He admonishes Ezekiel not to be afraid of them—even as He warns him that they will not "harken" to his words. He gives Ezekiel a "roll of a book," that is full of "lamentations, and mourning, and woe," and tells him to eat it. In his mouth, the book is as sweet as honey (just as a similar book was in the mouth of John the Revelator).[120] Finally, the Lord proclaims Ezekiel's charge and responsibility—to preach repentance to the children of Israel. (It's interesting to note that the Lord told Ezekiel at this point that if He

[118] Revelation 4:7. [120] Revelation 10:9.
[119] Doctrine & Covenants 77:2–4.

had sent him to those *not* of the house of Israel, they would have harkened to his words and repented, but that the Israelites would not.) The Lord then explains His charge by telling Ezekiel, "Son of man, I have made thee a watchman unto the house of Israel: therefore . . . give them warning from me. When I say unto the wicked, Thou shalt surely die; and thou givest him not warning, nor speakest to warn the wicked from his wicked way, to save his life; the same wicked man shall die in his iniquity; *but his blood will I require at thine hand.* Yet if thou warn the wicked, and he turn not from his wickedness, nor from his wicked way, he shall die in his iniquity; *but thou hast delivered thy soul.*" (Emphasis added.) This important doctrine is known as the *Ezekiel Doctrine*, and is reiterated and expanded by the Lord in Chapters 18 and 33 of Ezekiel.)

The Ezekiel Doctrine is a doctrine that involves both the teacher and the people. The teacher must teach and warn the people. If he does, the people are responsible for their own sins and the teacher has fulfilled his calling and "delivered his soul." If, however, the teacher *doesn't* warn the people, then the sins of the people are upon the teacher. The people, once taught and if they are in sin, have the opportunity to repent. If they remain in sin their soul is lost, but if they repent, all their former sins are forgiven and they have delivered their souls. If they are righteous and remain righteous their souls are saved, but if they are righteous and turn to sin, all their righteousness is forgotten and their souls are lost. It's a tough—but fair—doctrine of judgment.

Ezekiel, like Jeremiah and Isaiah before him, is another "show and tell" prophet. He was commanded to perform certain actions that would "show and tell" Israel what the Lord had in mind for them. He was to lay on his left side three hundred and ninety days to bear the iniquity of the house of Israel. "For," said the Lord, "I have laid upon thee the years of their iniquity." He was then to lay on his right side forty days to bear the iniquity of the house of Judah, "each day for a year." Thereafter, he was to bake barley cakes and drink water in careful measurements. This analogy represented the limited nourishment that would be available when the final siege of Jerusalem brought famine to its inhabitants. Then he was told to cut his hair and beard, burn a third of it, chop a third part of it with a knife, and scatter a third part of it to the wind. This was a representation of what would happen to the Jews during and after the siege of Jerusalem: a third would be consumed with pestilence and famine, a third would fall by the sword, and a third would be scattered in the diaspora.

The Lord was angry with Judah for her disobedience and He asked Ezekiel if he had seen what the people did in the "dark," (signifying that the people thought the Lord would not discover their sins). He showed Ezekiel women weeping for false gods and men worshiping the sun while in the temple. These sins and others would cause the Lord to bring destruction upon the people, and the devastation Ezekiel saw in his vision was so great that he asked the Lord if He would destroy "all the residue of Israel?" The Lord responded on a more positive note by telling Ezekiel that He would eventually gather the remnants of Israel from among the various countries in which they had been scattered and bring them back to the promised land.

These prophecies of destruction and judgment aimed at Judah and Jerusalem continue throughout the first twenty-four chapters of Ezekiel. As in Jeremiah, they explicitly express the Lord's anger with the iniquity-laden Israelites and they prophesy of their destruction and captivity before those events occur. The balance of the chapters were written after the people were taken into captivity.

Chapters 25–32 contain a group of prophecies, judgments, and punishments that involve the seven nations that surround Israel. (Jeremiah also delivered these prophecies.) Chapters 33–39 deal with the gathering and restoration of Israel. Two very interesting things are found in Chapter 37: Ezekiel's famous vision of "D'm" bones wherein a long dead army's bones are gathered together and reconnected to teach the prophet about the gathering of Israel (and to provide a similitude of the resurrection); and his instruction from the Lord to write upon two "sticks," one for Judah (representing the Bible), and one for Joseph (representing the Book of Mormon), noting that "they shall become one in thine hand." The balance of Ezekiel's book, Chapters 40–48, deals with the reconstruction of the temple in Jerusalem and the Israelites' worship ceremonies.

There are two general cross references to Ezekiel in the New Testament, but not a single quote. However, the authenticity of Ezekiel's writings was substantiated in the latter days when the Lord confirmed that Ezekiel was speaking of the fall of the great and abominable church. The Lord said this church would be "cast down by devouring fire, according as it is spoken by the mouth of Ezekiel the prophet, who spoke of these things, which have not come to pass but surely must."[121]

The only personal information we have about Ezekiel is that he was married and that his wife died while they were in captivity. Traditionally, it is believed that he died in exile and was buried near the Euphrates River.

Section VI
After the Captivity

After their return from captivity by the Babylonians, the people of the Southern Kingdom are referred to as the Kingdom of Judah. The Northern Kingdom had been destroyed for more than two hundred years, and from the return from captivity until the time of Christ, there was only one kingdom. All of the children of Israel at this point, regardless of their tribe, are collectively referred to as "Jews." No king ruled the Kingdom of Judah thereafter.

Ezra

536–443 B.C.
Book of Ezra

The book of Ezra is a continuation of the history recorded in First and Second Chronicles, and Nehemiah is a continuation of the history as written in Ezra. The two books—Ezra and Nehemiah—are considered one book by the Jews.

Ezra and Nehemiah worked together to free the Jews from their captivity in Babylon and return them to Jerusalem. Their objectives were to rebuild the temple, rebuild the walls of Jerusalem, restore the city of Jerusalem itself, and reestablish the law of the Lord and its proper worship by the people. The prophets Haggai and Zechariah were also ministering to them and to the people during this same time period. (Although it's not mentioned in either book, Daniel is still alive and serving in the Persian court of King Cyrus and continued up to the third year of his reign.)

In the first six chapters of Ezra a man named Zerubbabel, who was the senior prince of Judah at the close of the captivity, devoted his efforts to taking all of the Babylonian captives who would go with him back to Jerusalem. He also took the temple instruments (including the Urim and Thummim) that had been taken by Nebuchadnezzar when he looted Jerusalem between 595–570 B.C. Zerubbabel received authority to do this in the first year of the reign of Cyrus, king of Persia. All this had been prophesied by Jeremiah and Isaiah, including the identification of Cyrus by name.[122]   Zerubbabel's avowed purpose was to rebuild the temple at Jerusalem. This resettlement created animosity between the Jews and those who would later be called Samaritans. The people living in Samaria at the time were descendants from the transplanted inhabitants placed there when Assyria defeated the Northern Kingdom and carried off the ten tribes. These transplanted people had developed a worship of Jehovah similar to that of the Jews and wanted to help rebuild the temple. They petitioned Zerubbabel to this end, but his response was curt and to the point: "Ye have nothing to do with us." Thereafter the Samaritans did all that they could to prevent the Jews from rebuilding Jerusalem.

✦   ✦   ✦

The story of Ezra proper (whose name means *help)* doesn't start until Chapter 7 of his book. His lengthy genealogy goes back sixteen generations until it reaches Aaron, the chief priest under Moses. Ezra was a priest also, as well as a scribe. Perhaps he was the first of the group later known as *scribes* at the time of Jesus.

The Jews revere Ezra and credit him with great things, including the establishment of the Great Sanhedrin and the synagogue, and the accumulation and editing of much of the text of the Old Testament.[123]   The time recorded above (536–456 B.C.) is the historical period covered by his book. Ezra's personal history began about eighty years after that (in approximately 457 B.C.) when he received a letter of authority from Artaxerxes, king of Persia, to resettle Jerusalem.

Ezra declared that his purpose was "to seek the law of the Lord, and to do it, and to teach in Israel statutes and judgments." Upon arriving in Jerusalem, he discovered that many of the Jews had married outside Israel. He rent his garment, shaved his head and beard, and "sat down astonied." At the evening sacrifice, Ezra bowed before the Lord and confessed the sins of Israel. When he

---

[122] 2 Chronicles 36:22, 23; Jeremiah 25:12, 13;   [123] Smith's Bible Dictionary: Ezra.
Isaiah 44:28.

concluded he wept, as did the people that assembled with him, and they made a covenant to put away their strange wives. This was then accomplished in an orderly fashion and the book of Ezra concludes with a long list of those who had taken strange wives and had covenanted to put them away.

The next time we hear of Ezra is some thirteen years later in Chapter 8 of Nehemiah. In this chapter, the people are seeking him out so that he can teach them the Law from the books of Moses. The entire eighth Chapter of Nehemiah is a record of the instructions that both Ezra and Nehemiah gave the people from those books.

Nehemiah

445–433 B.C.
Book of Nehemiah

Nehemiah means *comfort of the Lord,* or *consolation of the Lord.* He was the cupbearer of Artaxerxes in the Shushan palace in the city of Shushan, the capital of the kingdom of Persia. He was appointed as the governor of Judea by Artaxerxes and served in that position during the historical period covered by his book. His lineage is from the tribe of Judah.

Nehemiah's principle task was to rebuild the walls of Jerusalem, reestablish the city to its former stature, and complete the reconstruction of the temple. His book gives us a graphic picture of the dilapidated condition of Jerusalem during his time. He was an ardent advocate of the Law and like Ezra insisted upon compliance with the covenant to put away strange wives so that the children of Israel could purify themselves before the Lord.

The rulers of the southern provinces of Persia near Judea plotted to stop the reconstruction of Jerusalem. To this end, they attempted to lure Nehemiah away from the holy city so that they could take his life. Although they did not succeed in these attempts, they were successful in convincing Artaxerxes to stop the reconstruction. However after some investigation, Artaxerxes allowed Nehemiah to continue his work. He soon completed the walls and dedicated them, and finished the needed repairs to the temple.

One of Nehemiah's social reforms was to stop the usurious lending practice being imposed upon the poor by the rich, and he refused a yearly salary when the salary was to be paid by taxing the people of Judea.

One of his religious reforms was to reestablish proper Sabbath day worship. He severely curtailed merchants from trading or even entering Jerusalem on the Sabbath by shutting the gates into the city from sundown on Friday until sundown on Saturday.

Other than the twelve-year span covered by the book that bears Nehemiah's name, nothing else is known about him.

Haggai

circa 520 B.C.

Book of Haggai

The name Haggai means *festive*. He was the first of the prophets to prophesy after the captivity of Judah by the Babylonians and was a contemporary of Zechariah. There is no record of which tribe of Israel he belonged to, nor is there any information about his genealogical linage or personal history–either factual or traditional.

Haggai's book initially consists of a rebuke of his countrymen because they have neglected the rebuilding of the temple (he was a contemporary of Zerubbabel). He also gave encouragement to Zerubbabel in the work he was doing to accomplish the rebuilding, and he exhorted the people to rekindle the worship of God in their public ceremonies. His book indicates that he was successful in these exhortations. He consoled the people because the reconstruction of the temple was visually less beautiful than that of Solomon's temple, but he promised them that in the future it would be restored to its former grandeur and more (this was fulfilled at the time of Herod the Great). He further prophesied in the name of the Lord that God would soon "shake the heavens, and the earth, and the sea, and the dry land . . . and [fill his] house with glory," perhaps anticipating the Second Coming.

Haggai's two-chapter book is short and can be read as a summation of what could have been a longer teaching. His final exhortation was to the people that they, as well as the priests, should eliminate uncleanliness from their lives and from their worship.

Zechariah

520 B.C.
Book of Zechariah

Zechariah's name means *Jehovah my righteousness.* He identifies himself as the son of Berechiah and the grandson of Iddo the seer (although Ezra declares him to be the son of Iddo rather than the grandson).[124] He was a contemporary of Haggai the prophet and served as a priest as well as a prophet. Along with Haggai, he directed much of his energy toward the rebuilding of the temple in Jerusalem and the return of the exiles from captivity in Babylon. He was probably born in Babylon and returned with the first caravan of exiles under the leadership of Zerubbabel.[125]

Zechariah was a visionary prophet, recording eight visions in the first six chapters of his book. His visionary expressions are like those of Ezekiel, Daniel, and John the Revelator since he writes the descriptions of what he sees in terms of symbols and allegories, leaving it to the reader to spiritually discern their meaning. His writings include two contrasting types of expression: one is straightforward, and similar to the exhortations of the prophets before him; the other is expressed in the obscure language of his visions.

Many of the visions and writings of Zechariah are similar to those of other prophets. His vision in Chapter 6 for instance appears to be the same vision that John the Revelator saw in Revela-

---

[124] Ezra 5:1; 6:14.   [125] Smith's Bible Dictionary: Zechariah.

tion, Chapter 6. He enumerates the sins of Israel in Chapter 7 of his book and in Chapter 8, he speaks of the eventual gathering of Judah and promises the Lord has made to her.

Zechariah Chapters 9–14 are both Messianic and apocalyptic. They are similar to (and should be read in conjunction with) Isaiah 24–27, Daniel 7–12, and Revelation 7–22. Isaiah, Daniel, and John appear to have received the same revelations and visions from the Lord that Zechariah did.

Nothing is known of the personal life of Zechariah other than that revealed in his book, and no specifics are given as to the length of his ministry or when his death occurred.

Malachi

430 B.C.
Book of Malachi

M alachi's name means *my messenger.* He is the last of the Old Testament prophets, but his prophecies probably belong to the same period as those of Nehemiah. He chastises the people in Chapter 1 of his book for their unfaithfulness. In Chapter 2 he directs that chastisement toward the priests and the leadership of the Jews, and identifies marriage outside the covenant to daughters "of a strange god" as the principle way the people are breaking their covenant with God. He warns the Jews against divorce from their "first wife." This *could* mean that they had given up wives of the covenant so that they could take strange wives, but it probably refers to the marriage similitude used by God on numerous occasions when He defines His relationship with the covenant people. In other words, they may have "divorced" themselves from their God. However, it appears that Malachi reverses this analogy: usually the Lord is the "husband" in His analogies and Israel is the "wife." Malachi makes the Lord the wife and chastises the people for putting God away (through divorce) so that they can worship the gods of their strange wives.

Malachi 3:8–10 uses the law of tithing as another example of how the Jews were breaking their covenants, yet the Lord promises he will "pour . . . out a blessing" so great "there shall not be room enough to receive it" if they will repent and live the Law. In

Chapter 4 of his book, Malachi begins with a single verse pertaining to the Second Coming and the vengeance the Lord will take upon the wicked, again ending with a promised blessing if they will yet live the Law.

Finally, Malachi prophesies of the future coming of Elijah in Malachi 4:5–6. This prophecy created the anticipation that still exists in Jewish tradition and is celebrated at Passover: that Elijah will yet appear before the coming of the Messiah. This anticipation was evidenced in the New Testament when John the Baptist was asked if he was Elijah which he denied, and it was again evidenced when Jesus asked the apostles who men thought that He was and they replied, Elias (Elijah), Jeremias (Jeremiah), or one of the prophets. However, it took the restoration of the gospel in the latter days before the prophesied return of Elijah was fulfilled.

Moroni first quoted Malachi 4:5–6 to Joseph Smith during his visit on September 21, 1823. "Behold, I will send you Elijah the prophet before the coming of the great and dreadful day of the Lord: And he shall turn the heart of the fathers to the children, and the heart of the children to their fathers, lest I come and smite the earth with a curse." The fulfillment of this prophecy occurred in the Kirtland Temple on April 3, 1836, when Elijah appeared to Joseph Smith and Oliver Cowdery and committed the sealing power and the "keys of this dispensation" to them.[126] These same verses from Malachi were also quoted by Joseph in an epistle on baptism for the dead that he delivered to the Church,[127] and in his history—where he noted that Moroni quoted the verses with slight variations.[128] The Lord himself noted the importance of this prophecy when he quoted it to the Nephites during his visit to the Western Hemisphere after his resurrection.[129]

Other prophets have also quoted Malachi on various occasions. For example, Christ quotes Malachi 3:1 as recorded in Matthew 11:10 when he refers to John the Baptist: "For this is he, of whom

[126] Doctrine & Covenants 110:13–16.
[127] Doctrine & Covenants 128:17.
[128] JS-History 1:37–39.
[129] 3 Nephi 25:5, 6.

it is written, Behold, I send my messenger before thy face, which shall prepare thy way before thee."

Nothing further is known of Malachi other than that contained in his book.

Section VII
The False Prophets

The first prophetic warning of false prophets came from Moses as he concluded his ministry. He called these men "dreamer[s] of dreams," and said that they might even be able to perform signs and wonders. He concluded that if they led the people away from worshiping the true God, they were false and should not be believed. Later, he even required false prophets to be put to death. It was also Moses who raised the question of how to detect a false prophet. His determination was: if a prophet makes a prophecy and it does not come to pass, then it is not from the Lord and the prophet is false.[130]

There are several instances in the Old Testament where a false prophet is specifically identified by name, but there are also many instances where false prophets are referred to but remain unidentified.[131]

---

[130] Deuteronomy 13:1–8.

[131] For instance see: 1 Kings 18:19; 22:5, 6; Jeremiah 23; Ezekiel 13:2.

Pashur Son of Immer

Jeremiah 20:1–6

Pashur was the chief governor in the house of the Lord and one of the ruling priests at the time of Jeremiah. The scripture reports that he heard the prophecies of Jeremiah which foretold that Babylon would conquer Jerusalem, destroy the city, and take the people into captivity. He brought Jeremiah before him and "smote" him and "put him in the stocks" that were located beside the Gate of Benjamin near the temple.

The next day Pashur brought Jeremiah out of the stocks—whether to confront him concerning his destructive prophecies or to further punish him we are not told. But before Pashur could do anything at all, Jeremiah spoke to him. He changed his name from Pashur, which meant *freedom*, to Magormissabib, which means *terror on every side*.[132] Then Jeremiah continued his destructive prophecies concerning Pashur: first, he would become a terror, not only to himself but to his friends as well; second, he would see the destruction of his friends by the swords of their enemies; third, Babylon would conquer Judah, carry the people into captivity, and slay them with the sword; and fourth, Jerusalem, its people, and its kings would be spoiled of all their treasures. Finally, Pashur and all his house and all his friends would

---

[132] Smiths Bible Dictionary: Pashur.

be taken in captivity to Babylon and would die there. All this because Pashur had prophesied lies.

Although we are not told what Pashur's lying prophecies were, we can reasonably assume that they were contrary to those of Jeremiah.

Ahab Son of Kolaiah, Zedekiah Son of Maaseiah, and Shemaiah the Nehelamite

Jeremiah 29:20–32

There are numerous places in the Old Testament where false prophets came in conflict with the prophets of the Lord. In Jeremiah, the people constantly ignored the prophet of the Lord, preferring the false prophets who told them what they wanted to hear. This led the Lord to declare: "The prophets prophesy falsely, and the priests bear rule by their means; and my people love to have it so . . . ."[133]

Ahab, son of Kolaiah; Zedekiah, son of Maaseiah; and Shemaiah the Nehelamite are three false prophets who were ministering at the time of Jeremiah. They prophesied falsely to the first captives who went to Babylon. Jeremiah had prophesied that the captivity would last for seventy years and therefore, the people taken captive should provide for that length of time by settling in, building houses, planting gardens, and providing for themselves. Apparently these three false prophets countered that information, indicating that the captivity would be much shorter and that the people should not settle in. Shemaiah even wrote letters appointing one Zephaniah (not the prophet) as a high priest in which he instructed him to arrest and reprove Jeremiah. The people believed these false prophets and their instructions.

---

[133] Jeremiah 5:31.

The Lord, through Jeremiah, told the false prophets Ahab and Zedekiah that they would be slain by Nebuchadnezzar before the eyes of the people (he roasted them in a fire). The Lord also told Jeremiah that Shemaiah would not live to see the "good" that the Lord would do among the people and that he would not have descendants.

Hananiah

Jeremiah 28

The Lord had commanded Jeremiah to place a wooden yoke around his neck to show the children of Judah that they would be put under hard bondage by Babylon during their captivity. Hananiah came to Jeremiah in the temple while he had this yoke on him and in the presence of the priests and the people, took the yoke off of Jeremiah and broke it, declaring that the Lord had broken the rule of the king of Babylon. He further stated that within two years all the people would return to Jerusalem, including the king's son, along with the vessels of the temple. Jeremiah only said "Amen" to this prophecy and left their presence.

Then the word of the Lord came to Jeremiah saying, "Go and tell Hananiah . . . Thus saith the Lord; Thou hast broken the yokes of wood; but thou shall make for them yokes of iron . . . I have put a yoke of iron upon the neck of all these nations, that they may serve Nebuchadnezzar king of Babylon; and they shall serve him." As for Hananiah, Jeremiah pronounced the condemnation of the Lord upon him stating that because he had caused the people to trust in a lie, he would die within a year. And he did.

Shemaiah Son of Delaiah

Nehemiah 6:10–14

Nehemiah was sent to be the governor of Judea at the end of the Babylonian captivity. He was also commissioned to rebuild the City of Jerusalem, repair the city's walls, and rebuild the temple. During this time several attempts were made by various enemies to lure him away from the city so that he could be destroyed. One of the attempts to destroy him was initiated by Shemaiah, son of Delaiah. He came to Nehemiah and told him his enemies were coming to kill him and to preserve his life, he should go with Shemaiah that night into the temple and shut the doors. But Nehemiah "perceived" that Shemaiah was not sent by God, but was sent by those who wanted him dead and was therefore a false prophet. There were others involved in this conspiracy against Nehemiah including, interestingly enough, a false prophetess named Noadiah.

Nothing else is known of Shemaiah or any of the other false prophets he was involved with, or of the false prophetess Noadiah.

Balaam

Numbers 22–25, 31

Balaam was the son of Beor and lived in Pethor by the Euphrates River. His story is unusual. It appears he was a well-known diviner who was endowed with the spirit of prophecy. His story began when the children of Israel were camped against the people of Moab for battle. Because of Israel's previous victory over the Amorites, the army of Moab and its king, Balak, were frightened; so King Balak, along with the princes of Midian, sent for Balaam to use his divining powers to curse Israel. The scripture notes that they took with them "the rewards of divination," which reveals that Balaam *charged* for the use of his gift.

After hearing the request from the princes (and presumably receiving his reward), Balaam retired to ask the Lord what he should do. The Lord communicated with Balaam. He told him that Israel was blessed and He prohibited Balaam from going with the princes. The princes returned to Balak and reported that Balaam would not come to him. Balak refused to give up and sent more honorable princes to Balaam—presumably with additional rewards. They offered Balaam anything he wanted if he would come with them and curse Israel. Again Balaam separated himself from the men and communicated with the Lord, and again the Lord responded. This time the Lord instructed him to go with the men, but he qualified His response by adding, "if the men come to call thee." (Perhaps the men had gone somewhere else to await Balaam's reply.) But Balaam didn't wait for the men to "call" him. He "rose up . . . and went with the princes of Moab" of his own volition, apparently yielding to the temptation of the riches and honor offered him—and this "kindled" the Lord's anger against him. It was on this trip to see King Balak that one of the most unusual stories of the Old Testament occurred.

God sent an angel (described as an "adversary") to Balaam to block the way of Balaam's donkey. The animal saw the angel and turned aside into a field. Balaam couldn't see the angel, so he smote the animal to get her back onto the path. The angel again blocked the animal as it passed between two walls. The animal "thrust" itself against one of the walls and crushed Balaam's foot. Again Balaam angrily smote the donkey a second time. Finally, the angel stood on a portion of the trail that was so narrow it would not allow the donkey to turn either to the right or to the left, so she "fell down under Balaam." Balaam became enraged and smote the animal with his staff a third time. Then the Lord opened the mouth of the animal and she spoke to Balaam. "What have I done unto thee," she asked, "that thou hast smitten me these three times?" "Because thou has mocked me," Balaam replied. As amazing as it is to have the animal speak, it is even more amazing to observe Balaam's reaction. He just spoke with the animal as if it were nothing out of the ordinary. In addition, he exacerbates his response by saying, "I would there were a sword in mine hand, for now would I kill thee."

But that's not the end of this amazing story. The conversation continued and when the animal provided argument and evidence of its loyalty to Balaam, reciting its long obedience to him since he acquired her, and asked if he could think of any disobedience she had tendered, Balaam responded, "Nay." At this point, the Lord opened Balaam's eyes so that he could see the angel—sword in hand—standing in the way. Balaam "bowed down his head, and fell flat on his face."

In time, Balaam reached his destination; but he blessed the Israelites instead of cursing them. However, he obviously learned nothing from his experiences because he later counseled the Moabites on the expediency of seducing the Israelites to commit fornication with the daughters of Moab. They did so and as a result, Israel was enticed by the daughters of the Moabites to worship their false gods—which brought the anger and punishment of the Lord upon the children of Israel. Finally, a battle was fought between Israel and the Midianites in which Balaam sided with the Midianites and was slain by the sword.

Conclusion

There are many wonders in the Old Testament. It is a record that can expand the mind and understanding of everyone who reads it. It also provides the foundation scripture for three religions: Judaism, Islam, and Christianity. It is evident from this examination of fifty-seven prophets that Amos was right, "Surely the Lord God will do nothing, but he revealeth his secret unto his servants the prophets."[134]

Just as the Old Testament is the foundation of these three religions, prophets are the foundation of God's work. From the beginning to the end of the Bible there were prophets—and we can be assured from this example that there will always be prophets.

There is really not an "Old" or a "New" Testament, but a Continuous Testament: prophets testifying, admonishing, teaching, prophesying, and revealing the word of God in an effort to direct His work. We only need to find and follow them so that we, through our obedience, may return to God's presence.

[134] Amos 3:7.

Chronology of the Prophets
References for prophets with books are in bold.

The Patriarchs

Adam	c. 4000 B.C.	Gen. 1:26–31; 2:7–25; 3; 5:1–5; Moses 2:26–31; 3:7–25; 4; 5:1–10; 6:1–12; Abr. 4:26–31; 5:7–21.
Abel		Gen. 4:2–10; Moses 5:17–35.
Enoch	3380 B.C.	Gen. 5:18–24; Heb. 11:5; Jude 1:14, 15.
Noah	2940 B.C.	Gen. 6:8–22; 7; 8; 9; Moses 7:42, 43; 8:12–30.
Abraham	2000 B.C.	Gen. 11:26–32; 12–18; 20–25:10; Abr. 1–3.
Isaac		Gen. 25:19–34; 26.
Jacob		Gen. 27–35; 49.
Joseph	1800 B.C.	Gen. 37; 39–48; 49:22–26; 50; 2 Ne. 3:4–21.
Israel's Bondage in Egypt	1690 B.C.	Gen. 15:13; Exod. 12:40; Gal. 3:17.

Prophets to United Israel

Moses	c. 1300 B.C.	Exod., Lev., Num., Deut.; Moses 1–2.
Miriam the Prophetess		Exod. 2:4–8 (Num. 26:59); 15:20, 21; Num. 12:1–15; Deut. 20:1; Micah 6:4.
Joshua/Oshea	1250 B.C.	Exod. 13:8, 16–30; 17:13–14; 24:13; 32:17; 33:11; Num. 14:30; 27:18–23; Deut. 34:9. Joshua.

Prophets during the Judges

Deborah the Prophetess	1130 B.C.	Judges 4–5.
An Unnamed Man of God		1 Samuel 2:27–36.

Prophets to Kings of United Israel

Samuel	Saul	1050 B.C.	1 Samuel 1–25:1, 28:7–20.
	David	980 B.C.	
	Solomon	950 B.C.	
School of the Prophets			1 Sam 10:11; 19:19, 20; 2 Kings 2:3–7, 15; 4:38; 6:1; 22:14; Amos 7:14.

Continued

Prophets of the Old Testament

Nathan — 2 Samuel 7:1–17; 1 Kings 1; Chron. 17:1–15.

Gad — 1 Samuel 22:5; 2 Samuel 24:11–19; 1 Chron. 21:9–19; 1 Chron. 29:29; 2 Chron 29:25.

Divided Israel — The Southern Kingdom (two tribes)

The following chart chronologically lists the prophets sent to the Southern Kingdom and the kings that ruled during their ministry.

	Rehoboam	Abijah (Abijam)	Asa	Jehoshaphat	Jehoram	Ahaziah	Queen Athaliah	Joash	Amaziah	Uzziah	Jotham	Ahaz	Hezekiah	Manasseh	Amon	Josiah	Jehoahaz	Jehoiakim
Shemaiah	✔																	
Iddo the Seer	✔	✔																
Azariah			✔															
Hanani			✔															
Jehu son of Hanani				✔														
Jahaziel				✔														
Eliezar				✔														
Obediah					✔	✔	✔											
Joel								✔										
Unnamed Prophets									✔									
Isaiah										✔	✔	✔	✔					
Zechariah										✔								
Micah											✔	✔	✔					
Nahum														✔				
Unnamed Prophets														✔	✔			
Jeremiah																✔	✔	✔
Zephaniah																✔		
Huldah the Prophetess																✔		
Habakkuk																		✔
Daniel																		✔
Urijah son of Shemaiah																		✔

The Southern Kingdom ended circa 570 B.C., after the Babylonian Captivity began. See the Reference Chart on page 194 for relevant scripture references.

Divided Israel — The Northern Kingdom (ten tribes)

The following chart chronologically lists the prophets sent to the Northern Kingdom and the kings that ruled during their ministry.

	Jeroboam I	Nadab	Baasha	Elah	Zimri	Omri	Ahab	Ahaziah	Joram	Jehu	Jehoahaz	Jehoash	Jeroboam II	Zechariah	Shallum	Menahem	Pekahiah	Pekah	Hoshea
Ahijah the Shilonite	✔																		
Man of God from Judah	✔																		
Old Prophet at Bethel	✔																		
Iddo the Seer	✔	✔																	
Jehu son of Hanani			✔	✔	✔	✔													
Elijah							✔												
Elisha							✔	✔	✔	✔	✔	✔							
Micaiah son of Imlah							✔												
Unnamed Prophets							✔												
Jonah													✔						
Amos													✔						
Hosea													✔	✔	✔	✔	✔	✔	
Oded the Prophet																		✔	
Hosea																			✔

The Northern Kingdom ended 721 B.C. See the Reference Chart on page 195 for relevant scripture references.

The Babylonian Captivity (circa 596 B.C.)

King	Prophets
Jehoiachin	**Jeremiah, Daniel**
Zedekiah	**Jeremiah, Daniel, Ezekiel**

The Return from Captivity (circa 525 B.C.)

Ezra
Nehemiah
Haggai
Zechariah
Malachi

Prophets of the Old Testament

Reference Chart
The Southern Kingdom, The Kingdom of Judah

Prophets of the Old Testament

Prophet		King	
Shemaiah	1 Kings 12:22–24;	Rehoboam	1 Kings 14:21–31;
	2 Chron. 11:2–4; 12:5–7, 15		2 Chron 9:31–12:16
Iddo the Seer	2 Chron. 12:15		
Iddo the Seer	2 Chron. 13:22	Abijam	1 Kings 15:1–8; 2 Chron. 13:1–14
Azariah	2 Chron. 15:1–8	Asa	1 Kings 15:9–24
Hanani	2 Chron. 16:7–10		
Jehu son of Hanani	2 Chron. 19:2, 3	Jehoshaphat	1 Kings 22:41–50
Jahaziel	2 Chron. 20:14–18		
Eliezer	2 Chron. 20:37		
Obadiah		Jehoram	2 Kings 8:16–24
Elijah (Translation)	2 Chron. 21:12–15		2 Chron. 21:1–20
		Ahaziah	2 Kings 8:25–9:29; 2 Chron. 22:1–9
		Queen Athaliah	2 Kings 11:1–20;
			2 Chron. 22:10–23:21
Joel		Joash	2 Kings 11:21–12:21;
			2 Chron. 24:1–27
Unnamed Prophets	2 Chron. 25:7–9,15,16	Amaziah	2 Kings 14:1–20; 2 Chron. 25:1–28
Isaiah		Uzziah	2 Kings 15:1–7
Zechariah	2 Chron 26:5	(Azariah)	2 Chron. 26:1–23
Isaiah		Jotham	2 Kings 15:32–38
Micah			2 Chron. 27:1–9
Isaiah		Ahaz	2 Kings 16:1–20
Micah			2 Chron 28:1–27
Isaiah		Hezekiah	2 Kings 18:1–20:21
Micah			2 Chron. 29:1–32:33
			Isa. 36:1–39:8
Nahum		Manasseh	2 Kings 21:1–18
Unnamed Prophets	2 Kings 21:10–18		
	2 Chron. 33:18		
Jeremiah		Amon	2 Kings 21:19–26
Zephaniah			2 Chron. 33:21–25
Huldah the Prophetess	2 Kings 22:14–20	Josiah	2 Kings 22:1– 23:30
	2 Chron. 34:22–28		2 Chron. 34:1–35:27
Jeremiah		Jehoahaz	2 Kings 23:31–34;
			2 Chron. 36:1–4; Jer. 22:1–12
		Jehoiakim	2 Kings 23:34–24:7
Habakkuk			2 Chron. 36:4–8
Daniel			Jer. 22:13–23; 26:21–23
Urijah son of Shemaiah	Jer. 26:20–23		
Jeremiah		Jehoiachin	2 Kings 24:8–17
Daniel			2 Chron. 36:9, 10;
			Jer. 22:24–30; 52:31–34
Jeremiah		Zedekiah	2 Kings 24:17–25:7
Daniel			2 Chron. 36:11–21; Jer. 39:1–
Ezekiel			10; 52:1–11

Reference Chart
The Northern Kingdom, The Kingdom of Israel

Prophet		King	
Ahijah the Shilonite	1 Kings 11:28–40; 14:1–18	Jeroboam I	1 Kings 11:29-39; 12:1-14:20
Man of God from Judah	1 Kings 13:1–32; 2 Kings 23:15–18		2 Chron. 10:1 - 11:4; 11:13-16; 13:2-20
Old Prophet at Bethel	1 Kings 13:11–32; 2 Kings 23:18		
Iddo the Seer	2 Chron. 9:29; 12:15; 13:22		
Nadab	1 Kings 15:25–31	Nadab	1 Kings 15:25-31
Jehu son of Hanani	1 Kings 16:1–12; 2 Chron. 19:2, 3; 20:34	Baasha	1 Kings 15:16-22, 27-29, 32-34; 16:1-7
Elah	1 Kings 16:8–14	Elah	1 Kings 16:8-14
Zimri	1 Kings 16:9–12, 15–20	Zimri	1 Kings 16:9-12, 15-20
Omri	1 Kings 16:16–18, 21–28	Omri	1 Kings 16:16 - 18, 21-28
Elijah	1 Kings 17–21; 2 Kings 1–2	Ahab	1 Kings 16:28 - 22:40; 2 Chron.18:1-34
Unnamed Prophet, and a Man of the Sons of the Prophets	1 Kings 20		
Elisha	1 Kings 19:19–21		
Micaiah son of Imlah	1 Kings 22:8–38; 2 Chron. 18		
Sons of the Prophets	2 Kings 2:1–18	Ahaziah	1 Kings 22:51 - 2 Kings 1:18; 2 Chron. 20:35-37
Elijah's Translation	2 Kings 2:11		
Elisha	2 Kings 2–13		
Joram	2 Kings 3:1–9:26	Joram	2 Kings 3:1 - 9:26
Jehu	2 Kings 9:1–10:36	Jehu	2 Kings 9:1 - 10:36
Jehoahaz	2 Kings 13:1–9	Jehoahaz	2 Kings 13:1-9
Death of Elisha		Jehoash/Joash	2 Kings 13:10-13, 25; 14:8-16; 2 Chron. 25:17-24
Jonah		Jeroboam II	2 Kings 14:23-25
Amos			
Hosea			
Zechariah	2 Kings 15:8–12		
Shallum	2 Kings 15:10–15		
Menahem	2 Kings 15:14, 16–22		
Pekahiah	2 Kings 15:23–26	Pekahiah	2 Kings 15:23-26
Pekah	2 Kings 15:25, 27–31; 16:5	Pekah	2 Kings 15:25, 27-31; 16:5
Oded the Prophet			2 Chron. 28:5-15; Is. 7:1
Hosea		Hoshea	2 Kings 15:30; 17:1-6; 18:9, 10

Prophets of the Old Testament

· · ·

The Lost Books of the Old Testament

Book of the Covenant	Exodus 24:7
Book of the Wars of the Lord	Numbers 21:14
Book of Jasher	Joshua 10:13, 2 Samuel 1:18
Manner of the Kingdom	1 Samuel 10:25
Book of Samuel the Seer	1 Chronicles 29:29
Book of Nathan the Prophet	1 Chronicles 29:29; 2 Chronicles 9:29
Acts of Solomon	1 Kings 11:41
Book of Shemaiah the Prophet	2 Chronicles 12:15
Book of the Prophecy of Ahijah	2 Chronicles 9:29
Book of the Story of the Prophet Iddo	2 Chronicles 13:22
Visions of Iddo the Seer	2 Chronicles 9:29
Book of the Iddo Genealogies	2 Chronicles 12:15
Book of Jehu	2 Chronicles 20:34
Sayings of the Seers	2 Chronicles 33:19
Book of Enoch	Jude 1:14
Book of Gad the Seer	1 Chronicles 29:29
Acts of Uzziah	2 Chronicles 26:22
Chronicles of King David	1 Chronicles 27:24

Some of these books may or may not have actually existed as separate works by separate prophets, but the references to them in the Old Testament indicate that additional records were used by the Old Testament writers as authoritative sources—especially the works of those prophets who are not only referenced by name, but who have some details of their ministry recorded in the chronicled scriptures.

The Prophet-Patriarchs Time Line

Although no absolute date can be assigned to many of the happenings in the Bible, and no beginning date is given when Adam and Eve left the Garden of Eden, it is interesting to see the time line that can be produced from the Garden exodus to the death of Joseph, which ended the Prophet-Patriarch period. The following chart provides the best information available from the Biblical record for this time line, assuming Adam and Eve left the Garden in 4000 B.C.

Event	Years	Scripture	B.C.
Adam's creation to Seth's birth	130	Gen. 5:3	3870
Seth's birth to Enosh's birth	105	Gen. 5:6	3765
Enosh's birth to Cainan's birth	90	Gen. 5:9	3675
Cainan's birth to Mahalaleel's birth	70	Gen. 5:1	3605
Mahalaleel's birth to Jared's birth	65	Gen 5:15	3540
Jared's birth to Enoch's birth	162	Gen 5:18	3378
Enoch's birth to Methuselah's birth	65	Gen. 5:21	3313
Methuselah's birth to Lamech's birth	187	Gen. 5:25	3126
Lamech's birth to Noah's birth	182	Gen 5:28, 29	2944
Noah's birth to the Flood	600	Gen. 7:6	2344
Flood to Arphaxad's birth	2	Gen. 11:10	2342
Arphaxad's birth to Salah's birth	35	Gen. 11:12	2307
Salah's birth to Eber's birth	30	Gen. 11:14	2277
Eber's birth to Peleg's birth	34	Gen. 11:16	2243
Peleg's birth to Reu's birth	30	Gen. 11:18	2213
Reu's birth to Serug's birth	32	Gen. 11:20	2181
Serug's birth to Nahor's birth	30	Gen. 11:22	2151
Nehor's birth to Terah's birth	29	Gen. 11:24	2122
Terah's birth to Abram's birth	70	Gen. 11:26	2052
Abram's birth to Isaac's birth	100	Gen. 21:5	1952
Isaac's birth to Jacob's birth	60	Gen. 25:26	1892
Jacob's birth to his move to Egypt	130	Gen. 47:9	1762
Jacob's death to Joseph's death	60*	Gen. 50:22	1685

* Calculated estimate:

Joseph being	17 when sold into Egypt	Gen. 37:2
	11** years a servant of Potiphar	Gen. 41:46
	2 years in prison	Gen. 41:1
Leadership in Egypt:	7 years of plenty	Gen.41:47
	7 years of famine	Gen. 41:54
	17 years Jacob in Egypt.	Gen. 47:28
	60 years from his father's death to Joseph's death	

Total: **110 years**

** Also Calculated

Alternate Routes for the Exodus

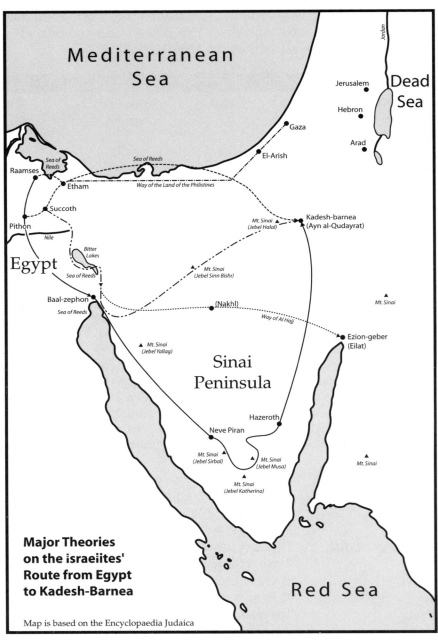

Mediterranean
Sea

Jordan

Jerusalem ●

**Dead
Sea**

Hebron ●

Gaza ●

Arad ●

Sea of
Reeds

Sea of Reeds

El-Arish ●

Raamses ●

Etham ●

Way of the Land of the Philistines

Succoth ●

Mt. Sinai
(Jebel Halal) ▲

Kadesh-barnea
(Ayn al-Qudayrat) ●

Pithon ●

Nile

Bitter
Lakes

Egypt

Sea of Reeds

Mt. Sinai
(Jebel Sinn Bishr) ▲

Baal-zephon ●

Sea of Reeds

(Nakhl) ●

Mt. Sinai ▲

Way of Al Hajj

Ezion-geber
(Eilat) ●

Mt. Sinai
(Jebel Yallag) ▲

Sinai
Peninsula

Hazeroth ●

Neve Piran ●

Mt. Sinai
(Jebel Sirbal) ▲

Mt. Sinai
(Jebel Musa) ▲

Mt. Sinai ▲

Mt. Sinai
(Jebel Katherina) ▲

**Major Theories
on the israeiites'
Route from Egypt
to Kadesh-Barnea**

Map is based on the Encyclopaedia Judaica

Red Sea